ROCK CLASSICS

ISBN 978-1-4768-1504-6

HAL•LEONARD®
CORPORATION
7777 W. BLUEMOUND RD. P.O. BOX 13819 MILWAUKEE, WI 53213

Visit Hal Leonard Online at
www.halleonard.com

CONTENTS

ALL RIGHT NOW

Words and Music by ANDY FRASER
and PAUL RODGERS

Moderate Rock

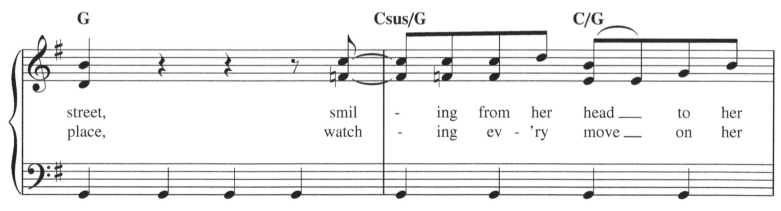

Oh, oh. ___

There she (1.) stood in the
(2.,3.) home to my

street, smil - ing from her head ___ to her
place, watch - ing ev - 'ry move ___ on her

feet. I said, "Hey! What is this?" Now ba - by, may - be,
face. She said, "Look, what's your game? Ba - by,

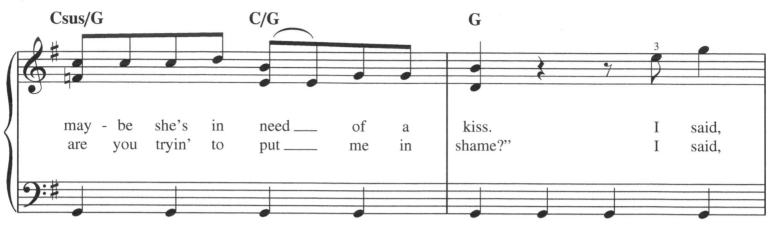

may - be she's in need ___ of a kiss. I said,
are you tryin' to put ___ me in shame?" I said,

"Hey, what's your name, ba - by? May - be we can see things the
"Slow, don't go so fast. Don't ___ you think that love ___ can

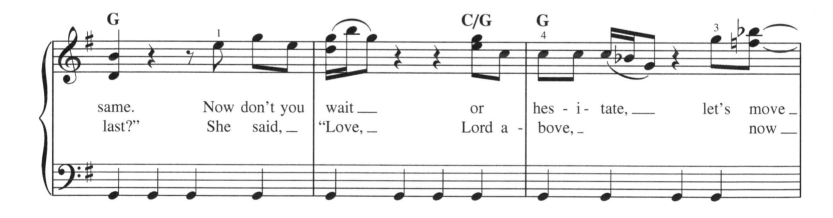

same. Now don't you wait ___ or hes - i - tate, ___ let's move ___
last?" She said, ___ "Love, ___ Lord a - bove, ___ now ___

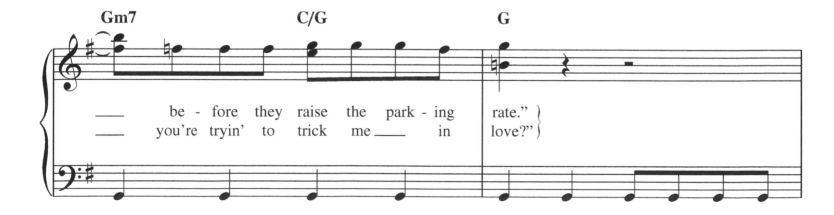

___ be - fore they raise the park - ing rate." }
___ you're tryin' to trick me ___ in love?" }

All right now, _ ba - by, it's - a al - right now. _

To Coda ⊕

_ All right now, _ ba - by, it's - a

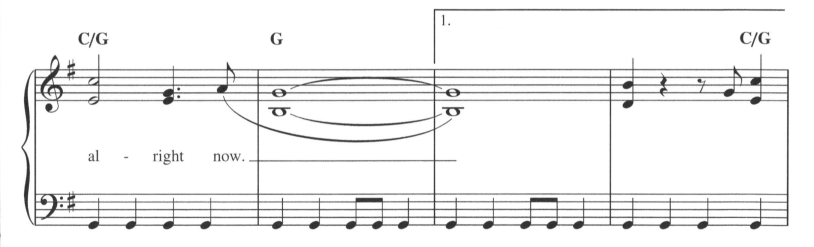

1.

al - right now. _

I took her

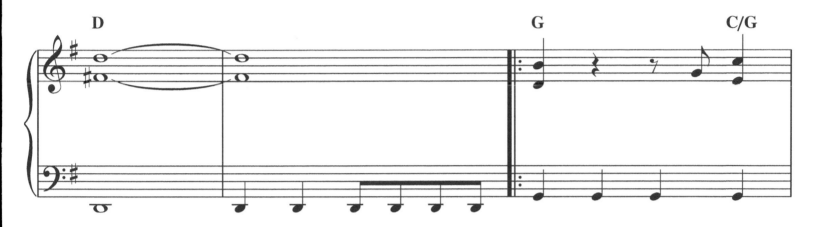

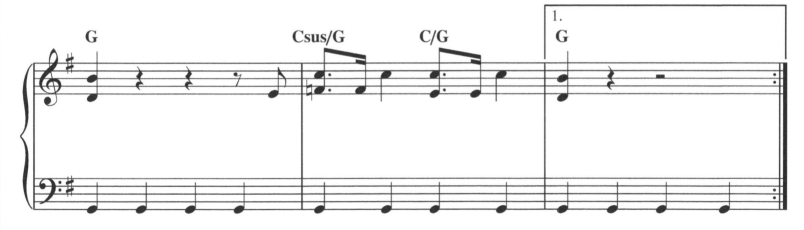

I took her

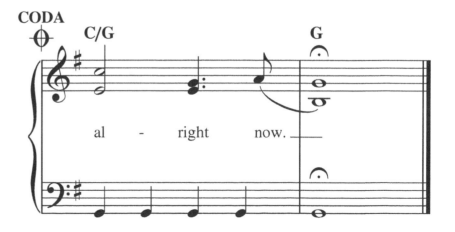

al - right now.

AQUALUNG

Words and Music by IAN ANDERSON
and JENNIE ANDERSON

Moderately

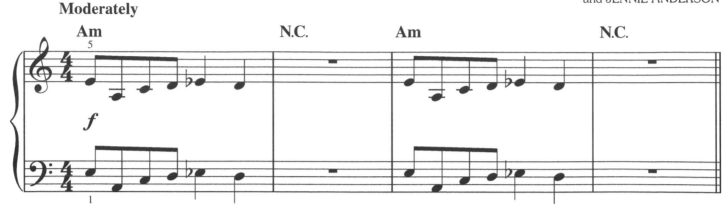

Sit - ting on a park bench, eye - ing lit - tle girls with

bad in - tent.

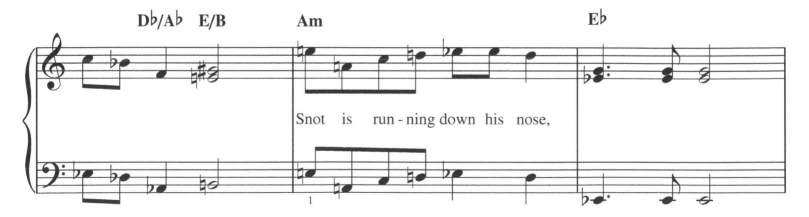

Snot is run - ning down his nose,

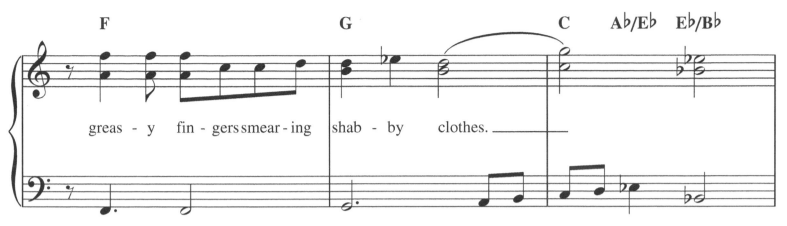

greas - y fin - gers smear - ing shab - by clothes. _____

Hey, Aq - ua - lung. Dry - ing in the cold sun,

watch - ing as the fril - ly pan - ties run.

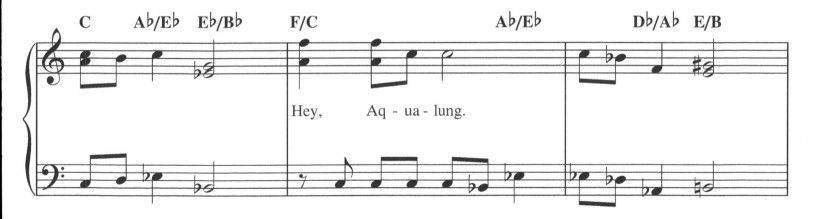

Hey, Aq - ua - lung.

Feel-ing like a dead duck,   spit-ting out piec-es of his

bro-ken luck.   Oh, Aq-ua-lung.

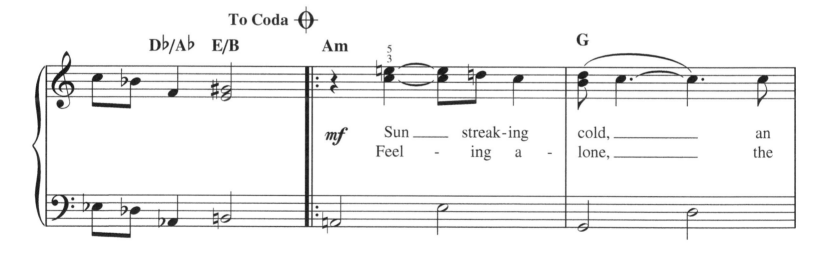

Sun ___ streak-ing cold, ___ an
Feel - ing a - lone, ___ the

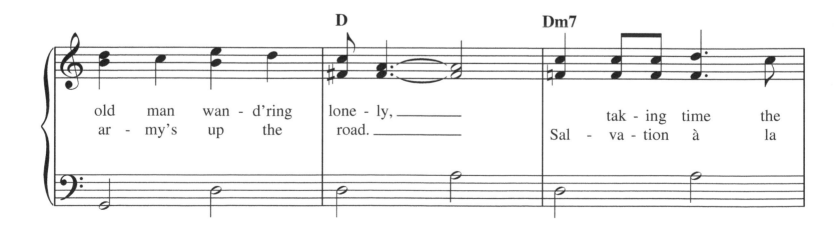

old man wan-d'ring lone - ly, ___ tak-ing time the
ar - my's up the road. ___ Sal - va - tion à la

2.

Faster

f Do you still re - mem - ber De -

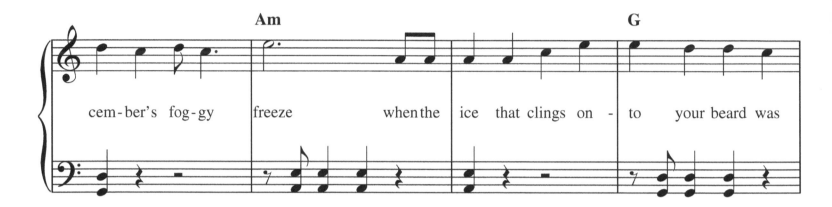

cem-ber's fog-gy freeze when the ice that clings on - to your beard was

scream - ing ag - o - ny? And you snatch your rat - tling

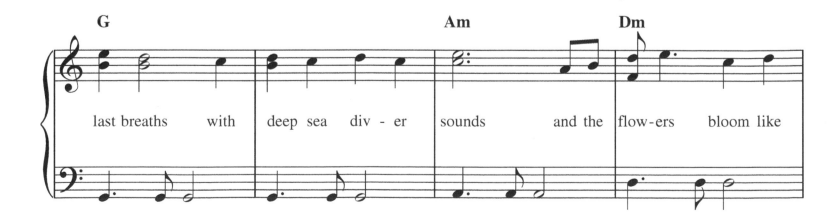

last breaths with deep sea div - er sounds and the flow-ers bloom like

mad - ness in the spring.

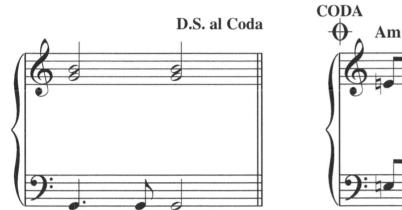

D.S. al Coda

CODA

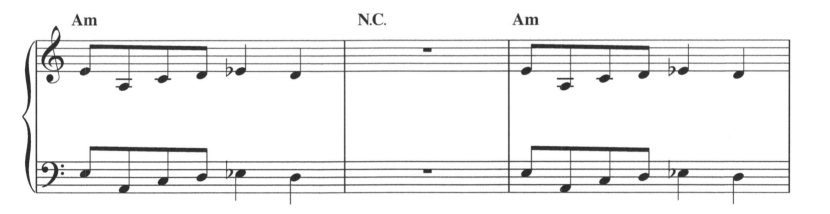

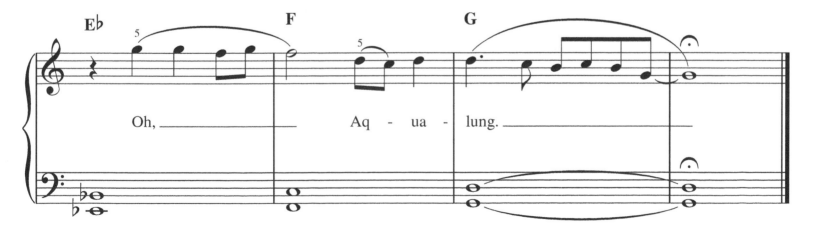

Oh, _____ Aq - ua - lung. _____

BABA O'RILEY

Words and Music by
PETER TOWNSHEND

With energy

Play 12 times

Play 7 times   **Play 7 times**

Play 4 times

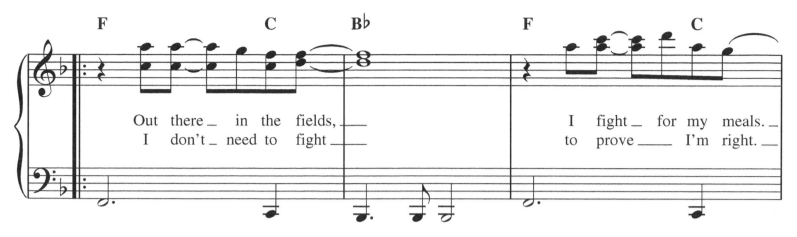

Out there __ in the fields, ___
I don't __ need to fight ___

I fight __ for my meals. __
to prove ___ I'm right. __

___
___

I get my back ___ in - to ___ my liv -
I don't need ___ to be ___ for - giv -

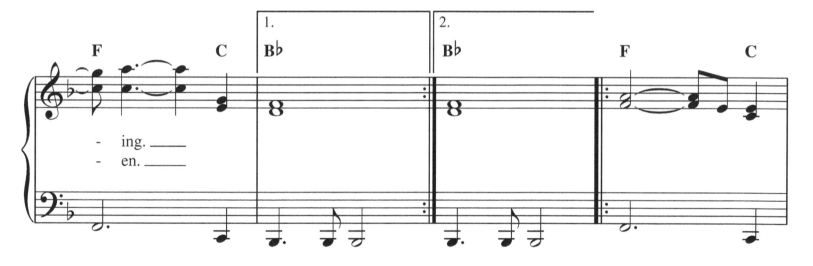

1.
2.

- ing. ___
- en. ___

Play 4 times

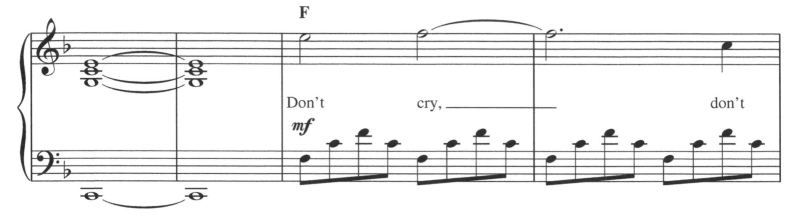

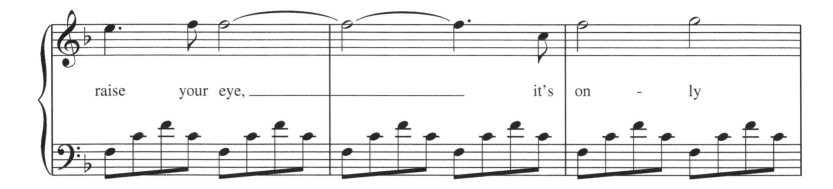

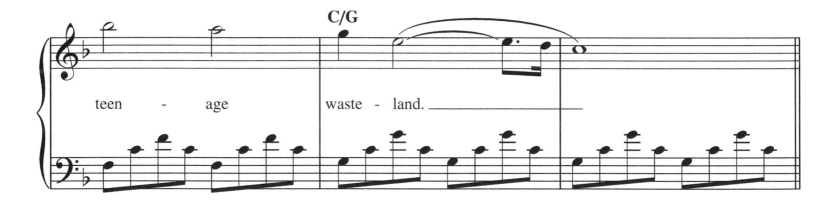

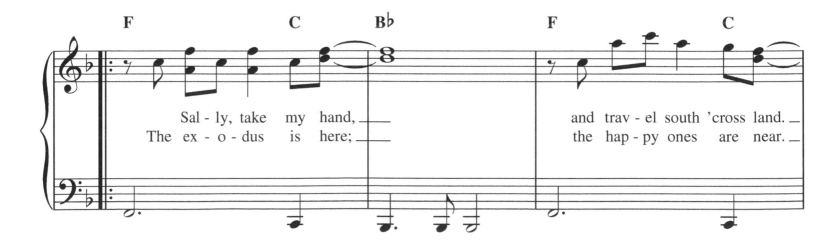

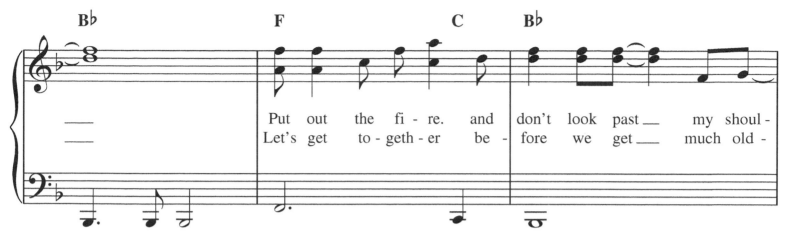

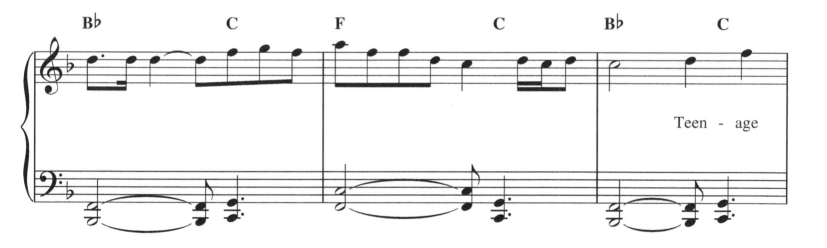

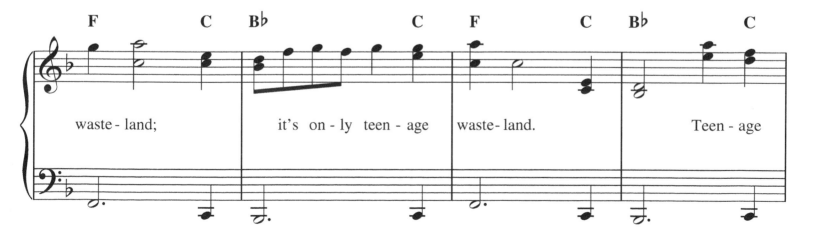

waste - land,_____ oh yeah._____ Teen - age waste - land.

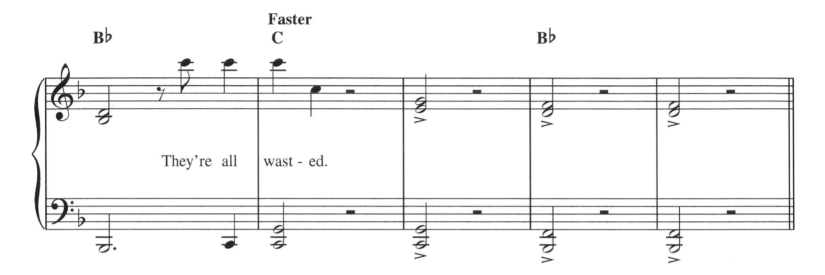

Faster

They're all wast - ed.

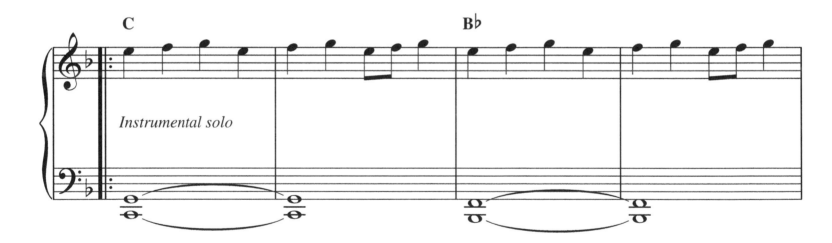

Instrumental solo

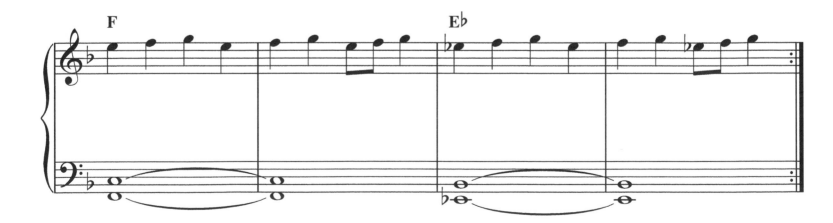

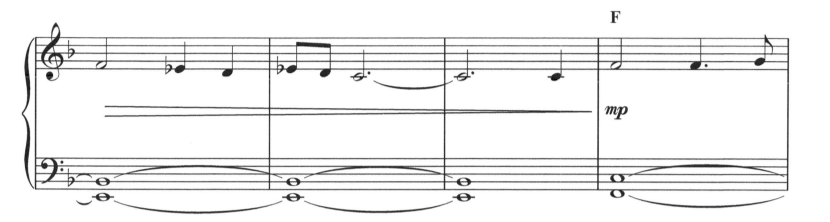

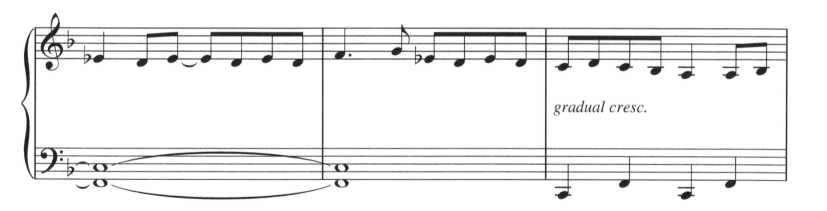

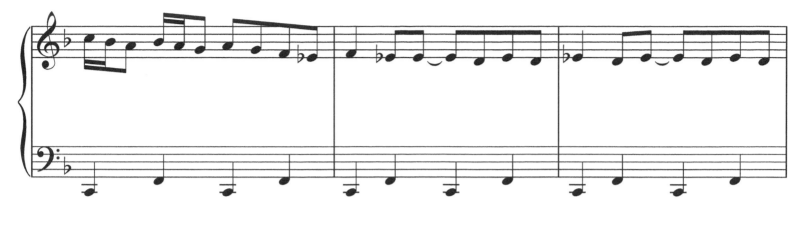

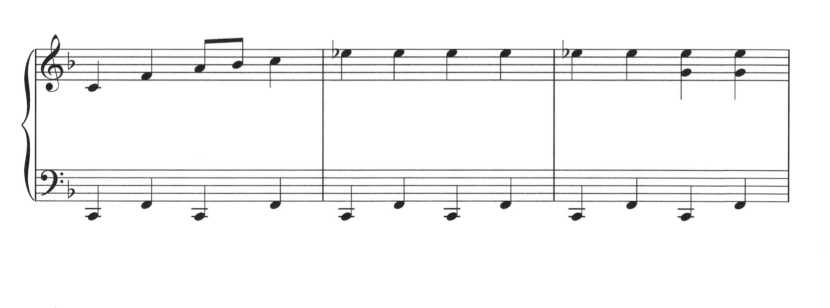

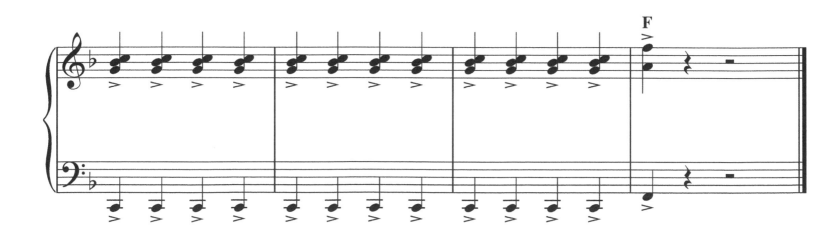

COMFORTABLY NUMB

Words and Music by ROGER WATERS
and DAVID GILMOUR

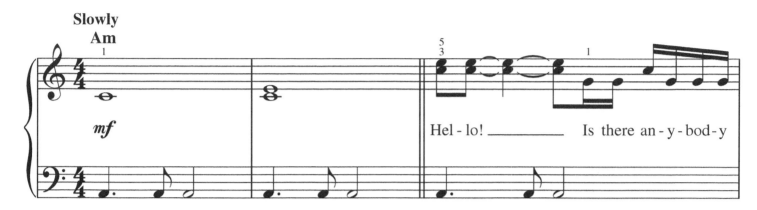

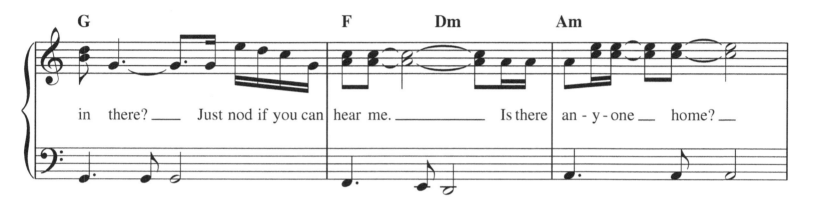

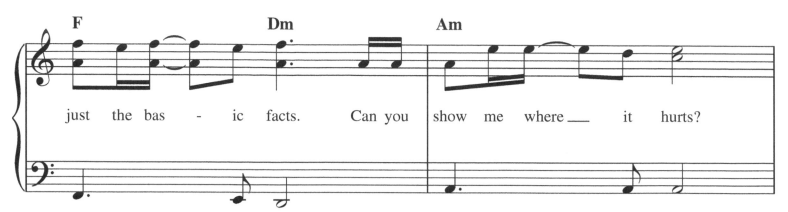

just the bas - ic facts. Can you show me where ___ it hurts?

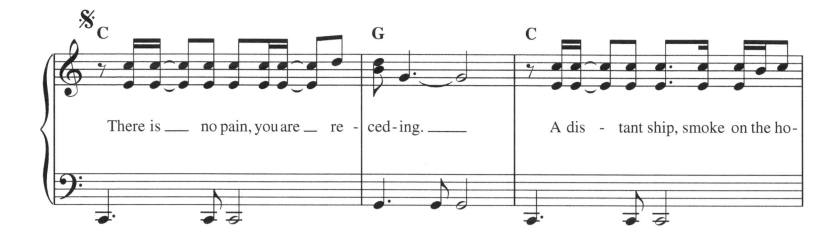

There is ___ no pain, you are ___ re - ced-ing. ___ A dis - tant ship, smoke on the ho-

ri - zon. ___ You are on - ly com - ing through ___ in

waves. _____ Your lips move, but I can't hear ___ what you're

25

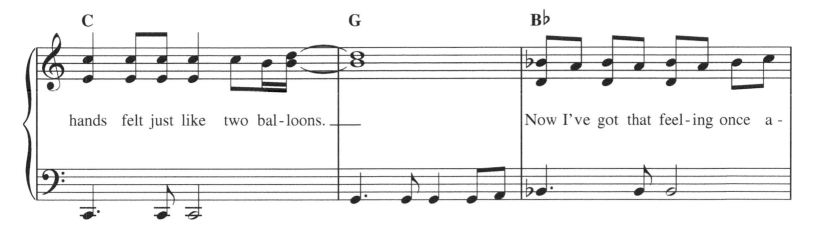

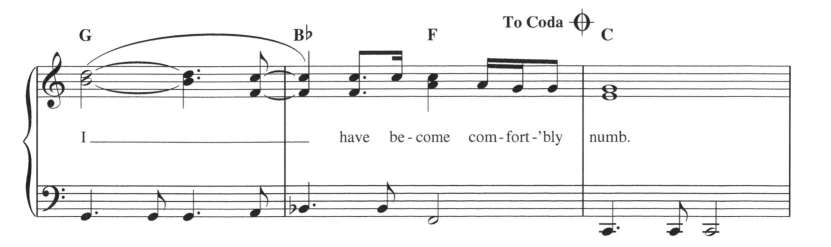

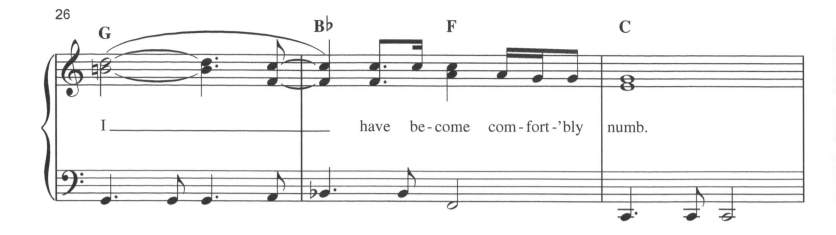

I _____ have be-come com-fort-'bly numb.

O - kay, __ just a lit-tle pin-prick. __There'll be no more "aaah!" _____ but you may

feel a lit - tle sick. Can you stand up? _____ I do be-lieve it's

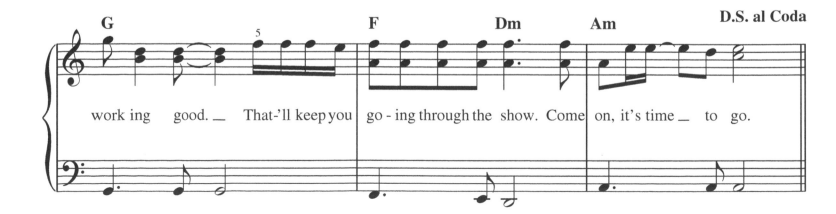

work-ing good. __ That-'ll keep you go - ing through the show. Come on, it's time __ to go.

CODA

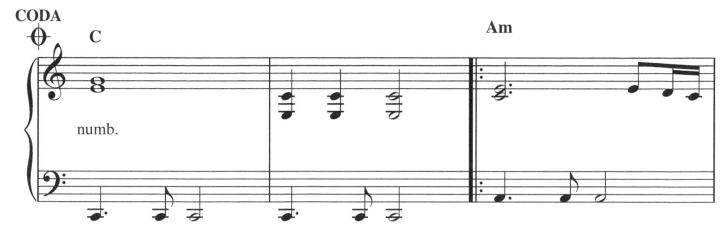

numb.

rit.

BACK IN BLACK

Words and Music by ANGUS YOUNG,
MALCOLM YOUNG and BRIAN JOHNSON

Heavy Rock beat

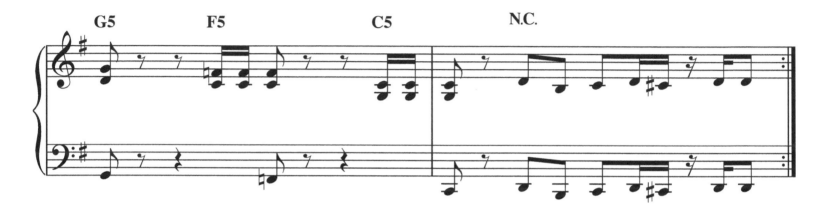

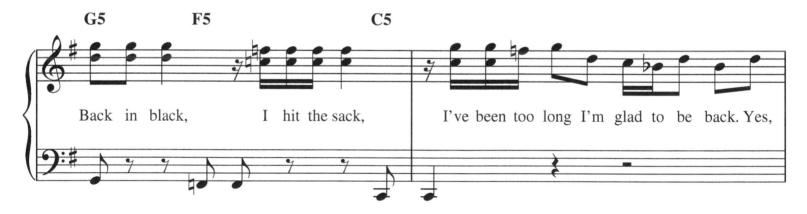

Back in black, I hit the sack, I've been too long I'm glad to be back. Yes,

I'm let loose from the noose that's kept me hang-ing a-bout. I keep

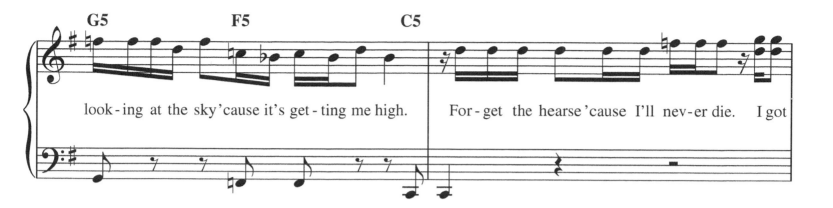

look-ing at the sky 'cause it's get-ting me high. For-get the hearse 'cause I'll nev-er die. I got

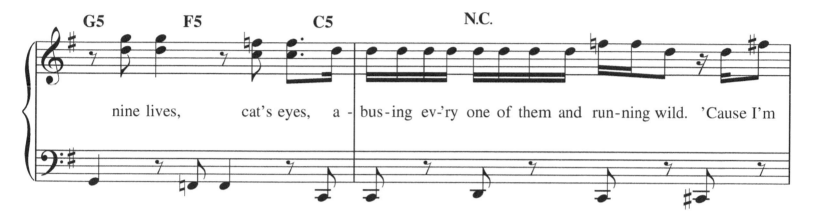

nine lives, cat's eyes, a-bus-ing ev-'ry one of them and run-ning wild. 'Cause I'm

back, yes, I'm back. _____ Well, I'm

back. Yes, I'm back. Well, I'm

back, _____ back. _____ Well, I'm

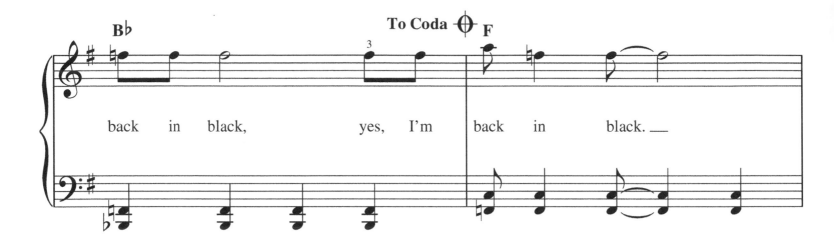

Bb   **To Coda** ⊕ **F**

back   in   black,   yes,   I'm   back   in   black. __

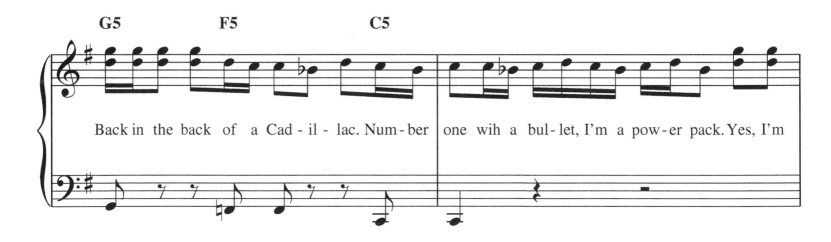

G5   **F5**   **C5**

Back in the back of a Cad - il - lac. Num - ber | one wih a bul - let, I'm a pow - er pack. Yes, I'm

G5   **F5**   **C5**   **N.C.**

in the band,   with the gang. | They've got to catch me if they want me to hang. __ 'Cause I'm

back on the track, and I'm beat-ing the flack. No - bod-y's gon-na get me on an-oth-er rap, so

look at me now, I'm just mak-ing my pay. Don't try to push your luck, just get out-ta my way. 'Cause I'm

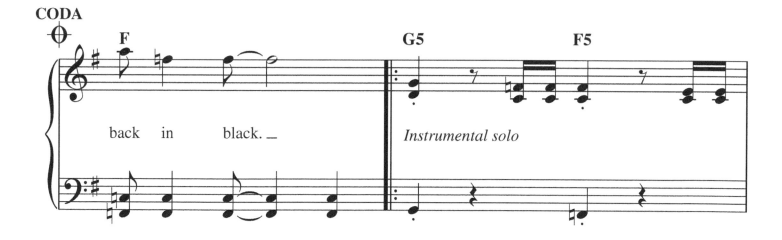

back in black. ___

Instrumental solo

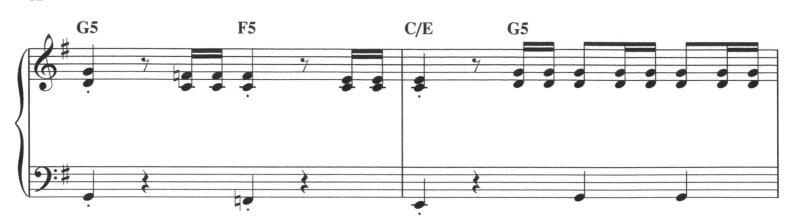

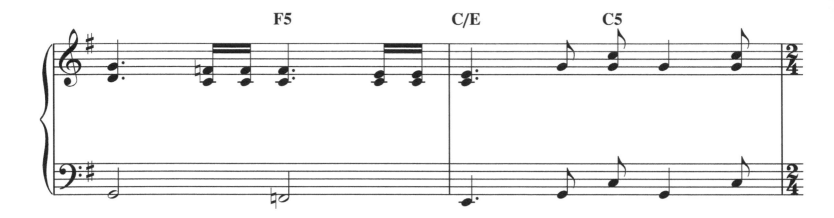

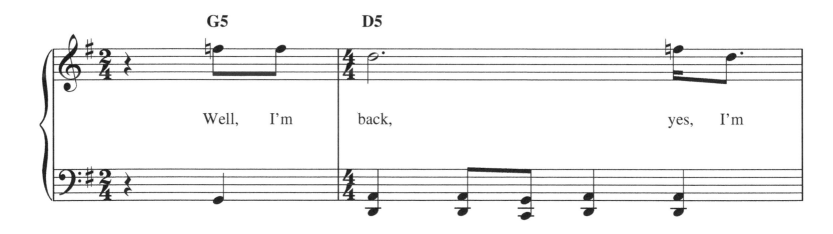

Well,   I'm   back,   yes,   I'm

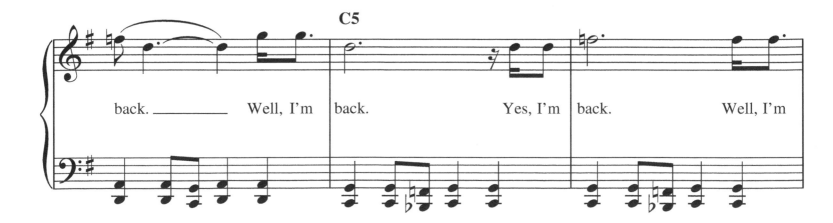

back. _____ Well, I'm back.   Yes, I'm back.   Well, I'm

back, _____ back. _____ Well, I'm | back in black, yes, I'm

back in black. __

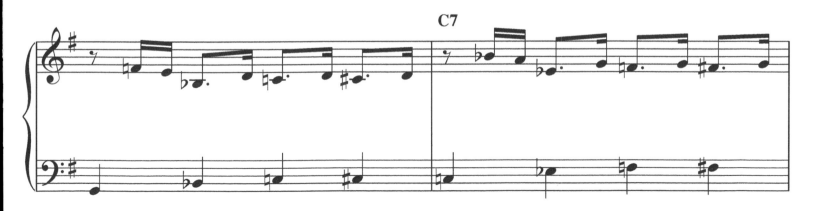

Back, _____

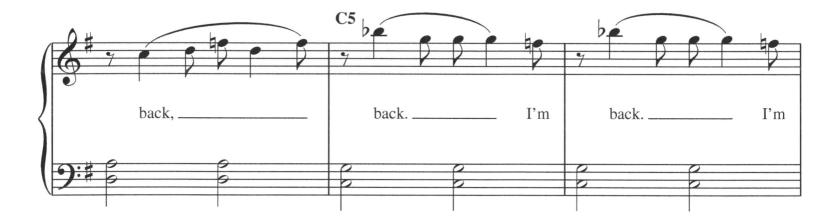

back, _____   back. _____ I'm   back. _____ I'm

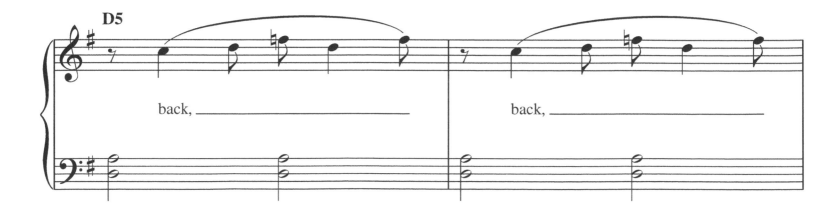

back, _____   back, _____

back in black, yes, I'm back in black. _

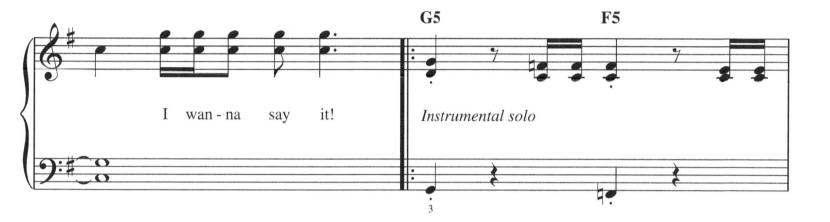

I wan-na say it! *Instrumental solo*

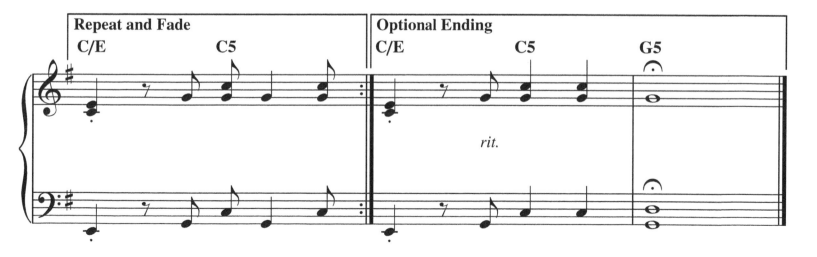

Repeat and Fade

Optional Ending

rit.

DREAM ON

Words and Music by
STEVEN TYLER

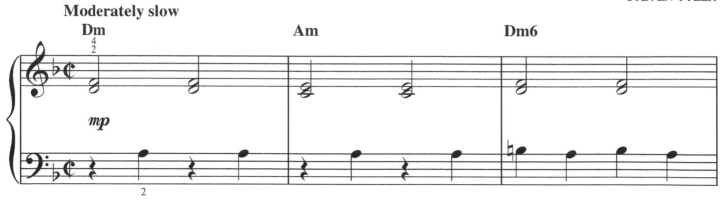

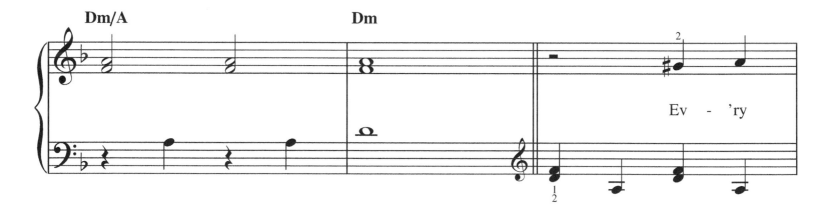

Ev - 'ry

time_____ that I look in the mir - ror,

all these lines on my face get-tin' clear-

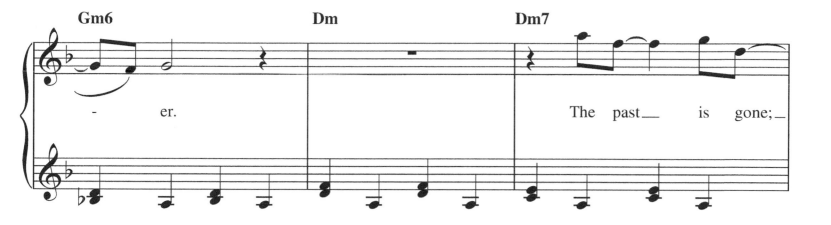

- er. The past___ is gone;___

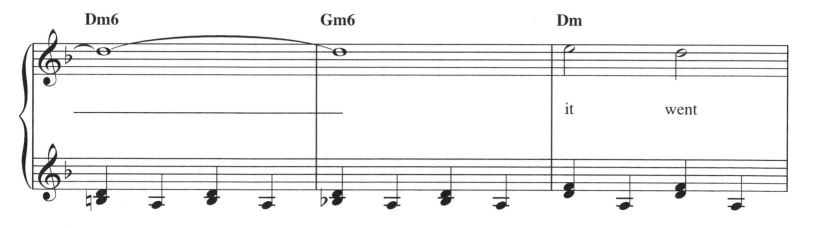

it went

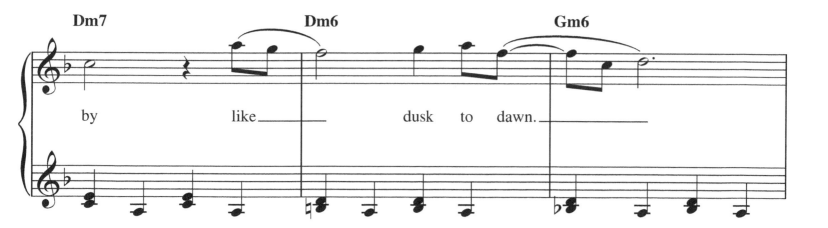

by like___ dusk to dawn.___

38

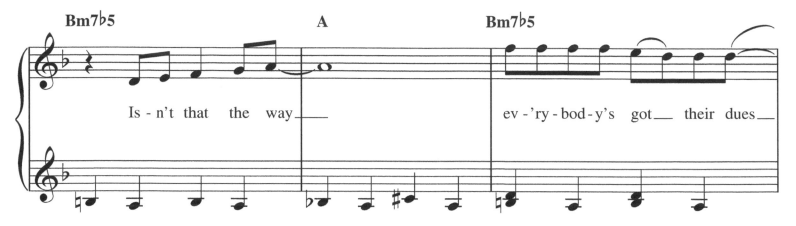

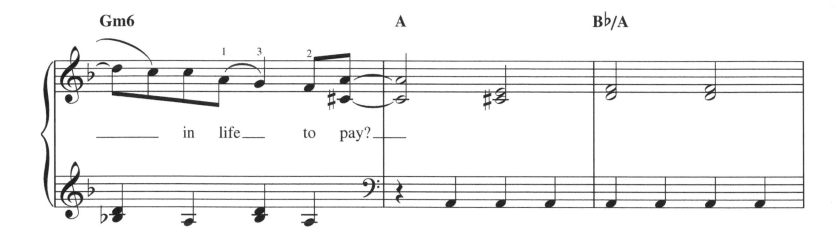

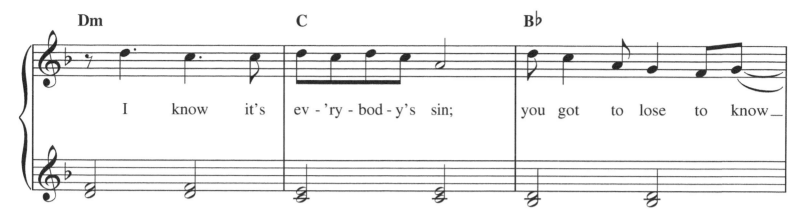

I know it's ev-'ry-bod-y's sin; you got to lose to know___

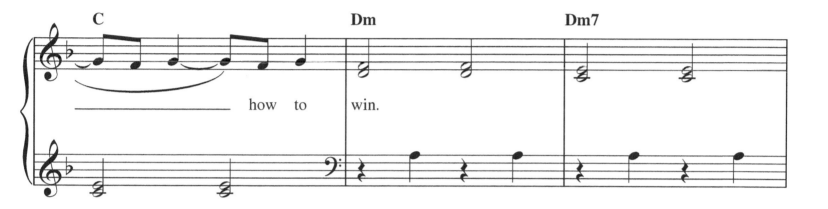

___ how to win.

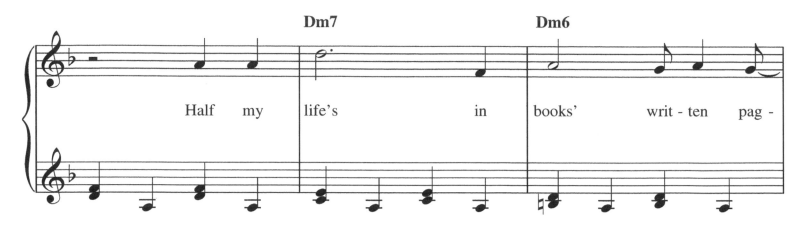

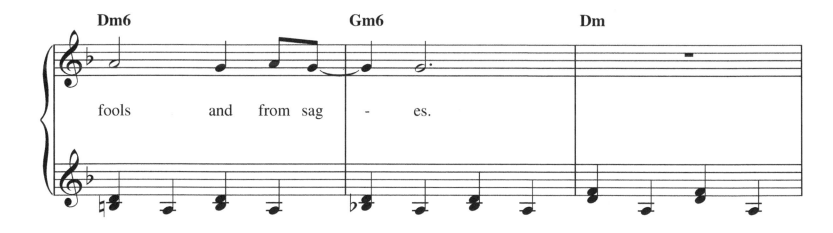

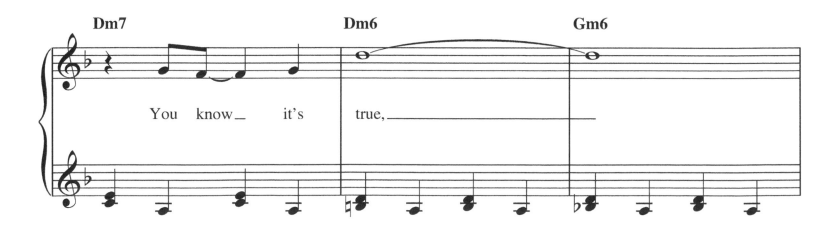

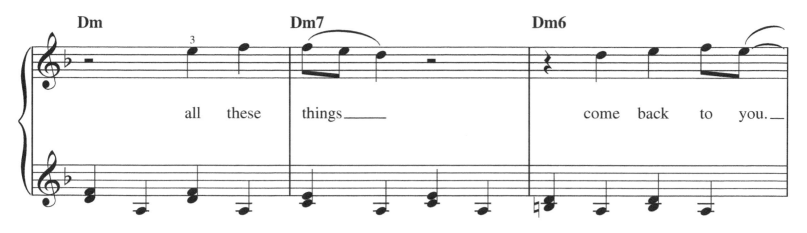

all these things_____ come back to you._

_____ Sing with me, sing for the years,_

sing for the laugh-ter 'n' sing_____ for the tears._ Sing with me if it's

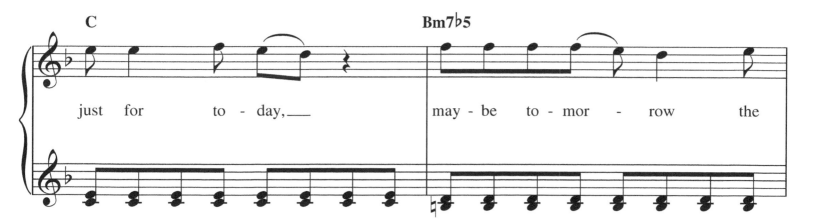

just for to - day,_ may - be to - mor - row the

42

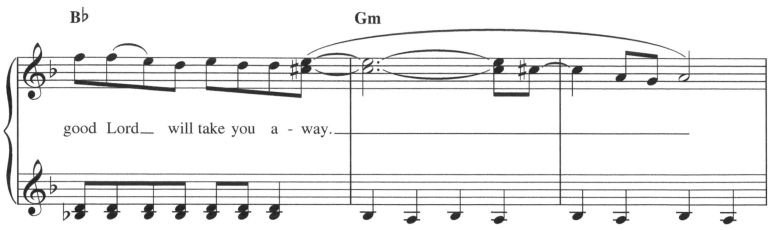

good Lord__ will take you a - way.__

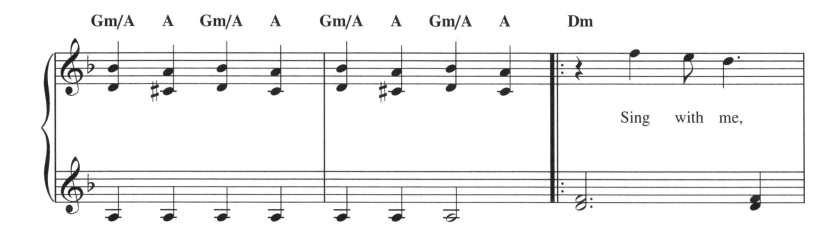

Sing with me,

sing for the years,_ sing for the laugh-ter 'n' sing____ for the tears.____

Sing with me if it's just for to - day,____

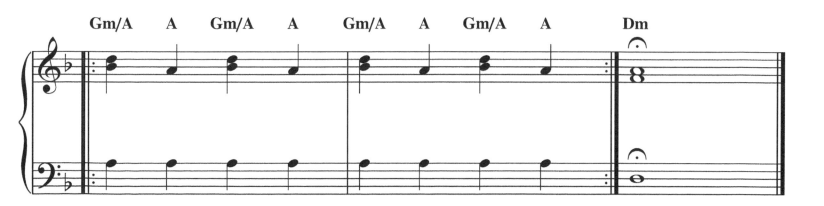

HOTEL CALIFORNIA

Words and Music by DON HENLEY,
GLENN FREY and DON FELDER

Moderate Rock

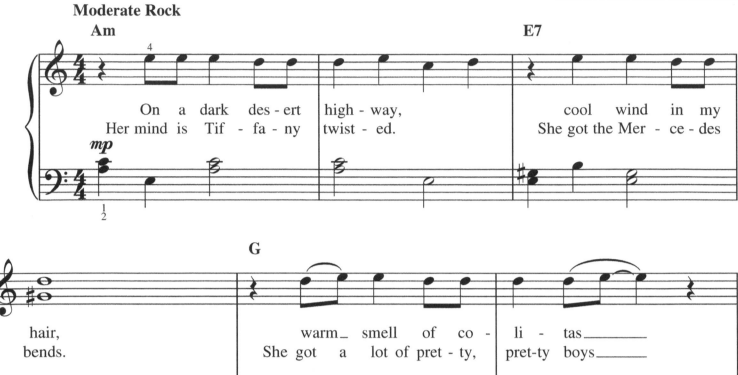

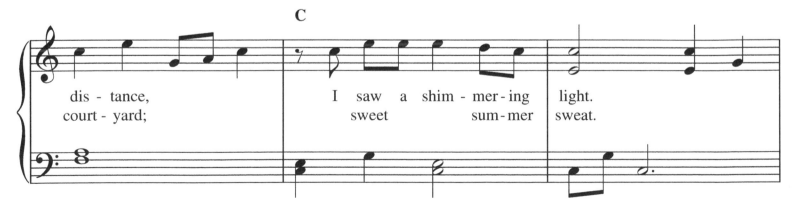

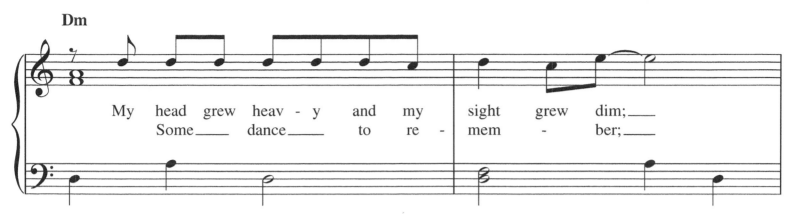

Dm

My head grew heav - y and my sight grew dim;___
Some___ dance___ to re - mem - ber;___

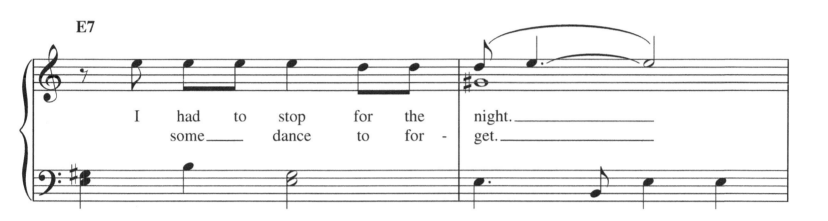

E7

I had to stop for the night.___
some___ stop dance to for - get.___

Am　　　　　　　　　**E7**

There she stood in the door - way; I heard the mis - sion bell.___
So I called up the cap - tain: "Please bring me my

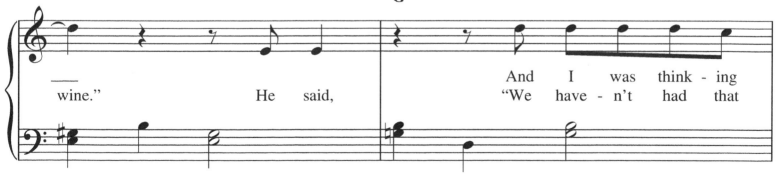

　　　　　　　　　G

wine." He said,
And I was think - ing "We have - n't had that

to my - self:___ this could be heav - en or this could be
spir - it here___ since___ nine - teen six - ty -

hell._____ Then she lit up a can - dle,
nine."____ And still___ those voic - es are call - ing from

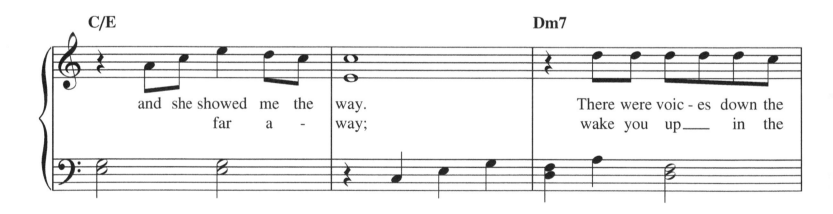

and she showed me the way. There were voic - es down the
far a - way; wake you up___ in the

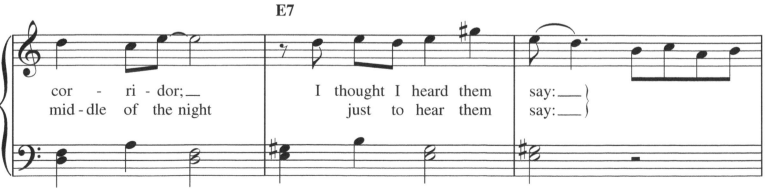

cor - ri - dor;___ I thought I heard them say:___ }
mid - dle of the night just to hear them say:___ }

F

"Wel - come___ to the Ho - tel Cal - i - for -

C   E7

- nia.   Such a love - ly place,___ (such a

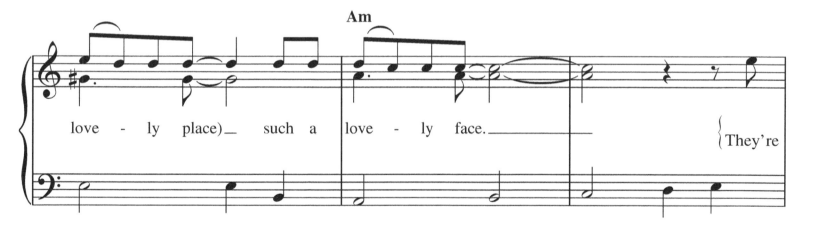

Am

love - ly place)___ such a love - ly face._____ {They're

F   C

Plen - ty of room___ at the Ho - tel Cal - i - for - nia.
liv - in' it up___ at the Ho - tel Cal - i - for - nia.

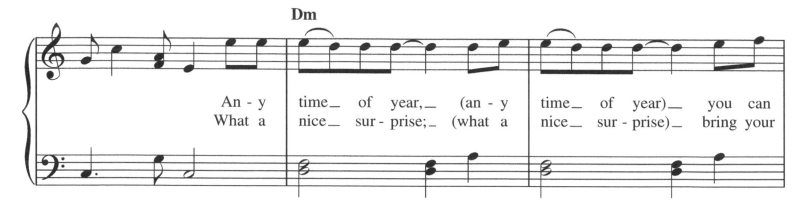

Dm

An - y | time of year, (an - y | time of year) you can
What a | nice sur - prise; (what a | nice sur - prise) bring your

1. **E**

find it here."

2. **E**

al - i - bis."

N.C.   **Am**

Mir - rors on the | ceil - ing,
Last thing I re - | mem - ber I was

E   **G**

the pink cham - pagne on | ice, and she said, | "We are all just
run - ning for the | door. | I had to find the

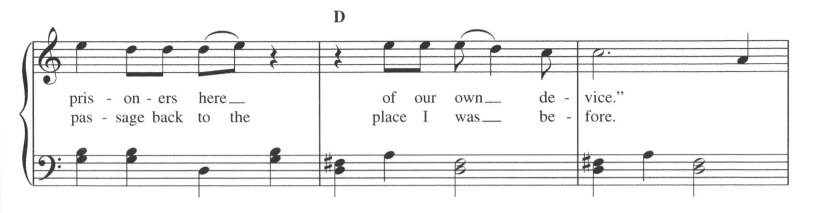

pris - on - ers here___ of our own___ de - vice."
pas - sage back to the place I was___ be - fore.

And in the mas - ter's___ cham - bers,___ they gath - ered for the
"Re - lax," said the night man.___ "We are pro - grammed to re -

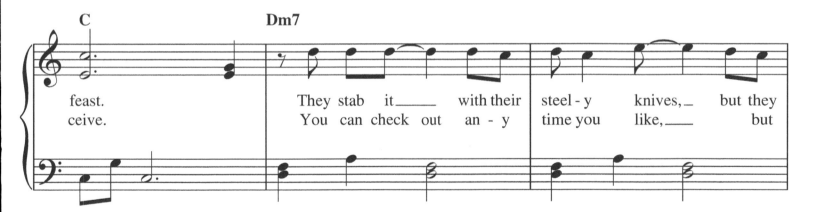

feast. They stab it___ with their steel - y knives,_ but they
ceive. You can check out an - y time you like,___ but

just can't___ kill the beast.
you can___ nev - er leave."

IRON MAN

Words and Music by FRANK IOMMI,
JOHN OSBOURNE, WILLIAM WARD
and TERENCE BUTLER

Heavy Rock beat

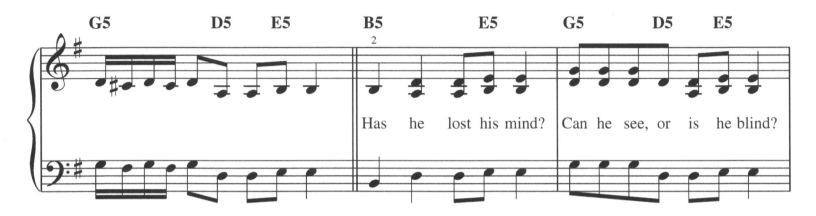

Has he lost his mind? Can he see, or is he blind?

Can he walk at all, or if he moves, ___ will he fall?

Is he a-live or dead? Has he thoughts with-in his head?

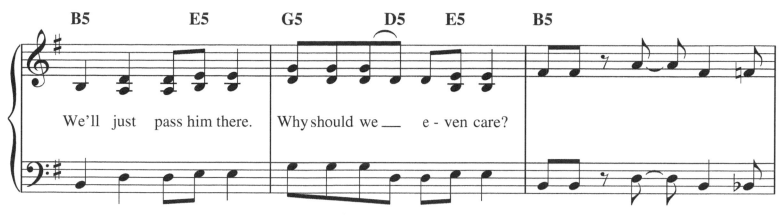

We'll just pass him there. Why should we ___ e - ven care?

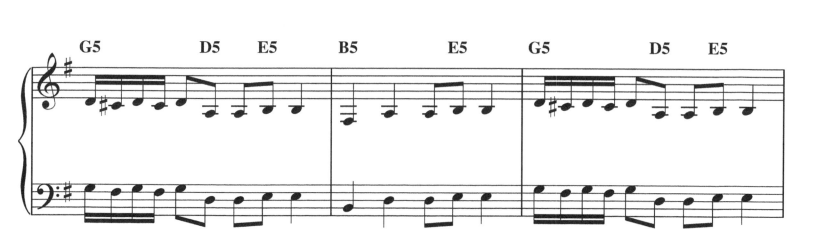

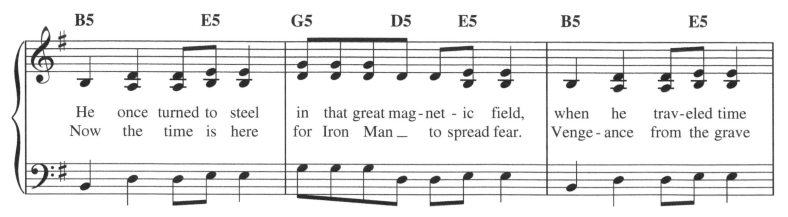

He once turned to steel
in that great mag-net-ic field,
when he trav-eled time

Now the time is here
for Iron Man __ to spread fear.
Venge-ance from the grave

for the fu-ture of man-kind.
No-bod-y wants __ him.
He just stares at the

kills the peo-ple he once saved.
No-bod-y wants __ him.
They just turn __ their

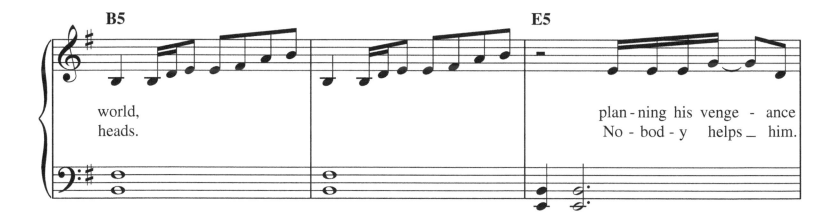

world,
plan-ning his venge - ance

heads.
No - bod - y helps __ him.

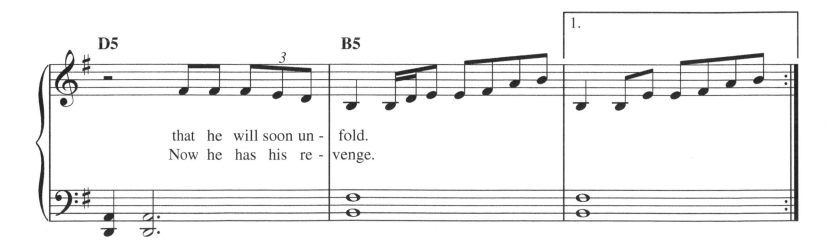

that he will soon un - fold.
Now he has his re - venge.

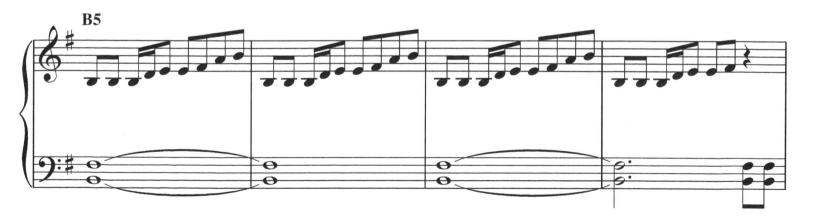

Heav - y boots of lead fills his vic-tims full of dread. Run - ning as fast as they can.

I - ron Man _ lives a - gain.

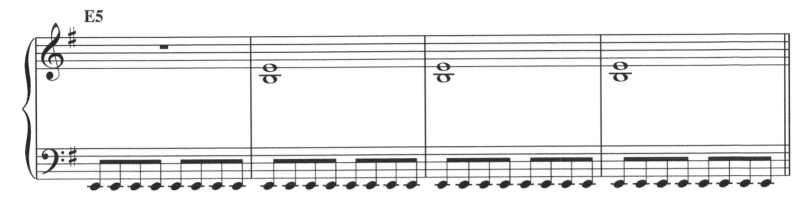

Play 5 times

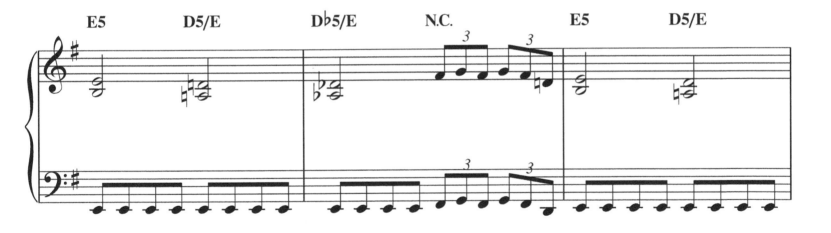

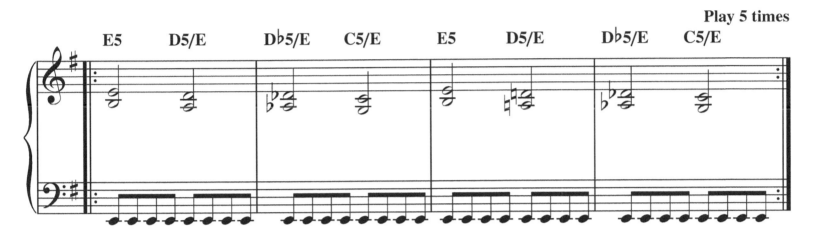

LOVE WALKS IN

Words and Music by SAMMY HAGAR,
EDWARD VAN HALEN, ALEX VAN HALEN
and MICHAEL ANTHONY

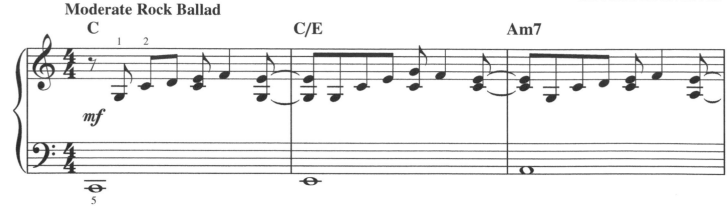

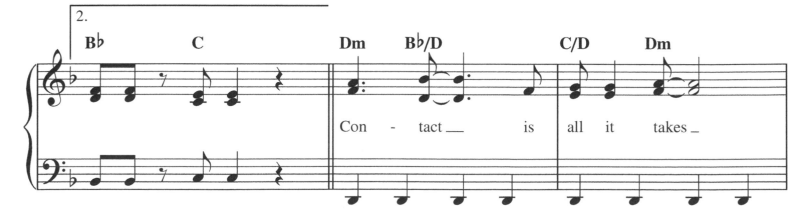

Con - tact ___ is all it takes ___

to change your life, to lose your place in time. ___

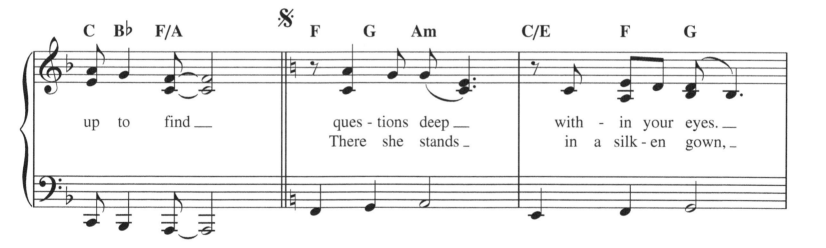

Con - tact, ___ a - sleep or a - wake ___ com - ing a - round, you may wake

up to find ___ ques - tions deep ___ with - in your eyes. ___
There she stands ___ in a silk - en gown, ___

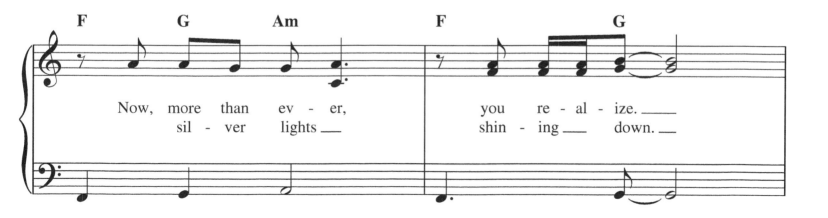

Now, more than ev - er, you re - al - ize. ___
sil - ver lights ___ shin - ing ___ down. ___

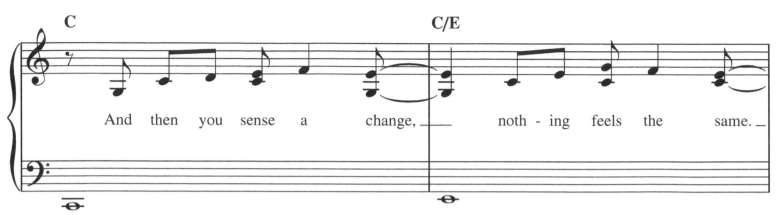

And then you sense a change, ___ noth - ing feels the same. ___

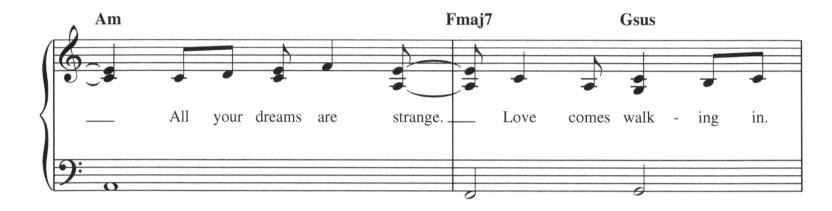

___ All your dreams are strange. ___ Love comes walk - ing in.

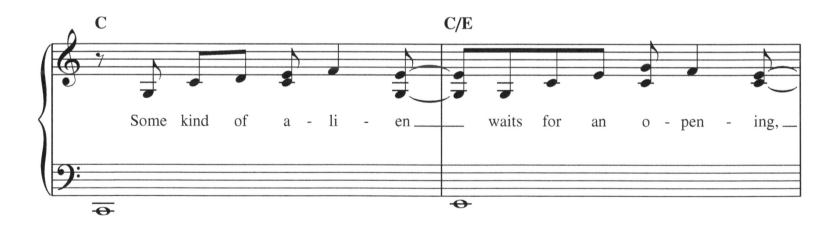

Some kind of a - li - en ___ waits for an o - pen - ing, ___

To Coda ⊕

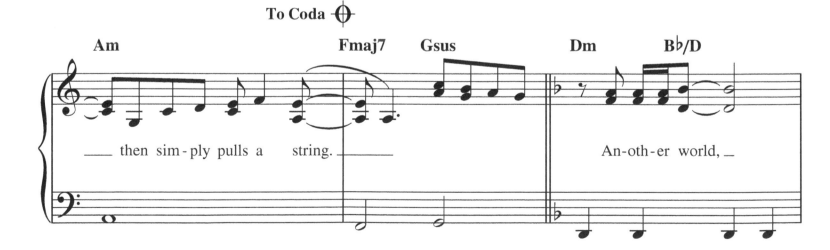

___ then sim - ply pulls a string. ___ An - oth - er world, ___

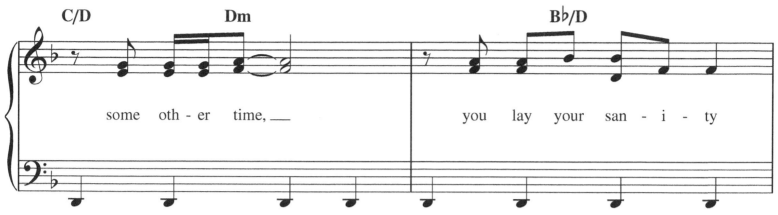

some oth-er time, ___ you lay your san - i - ty

on the line. ___ Fa - mil - iar fac - es, fa - mil - iar sights.

Reach back, re - mem - ber with all your might. ___

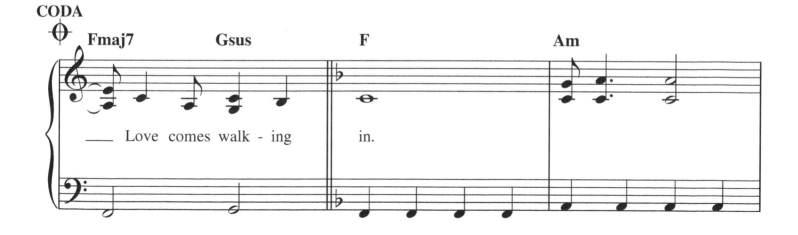

___ Love comes walk - ing in.

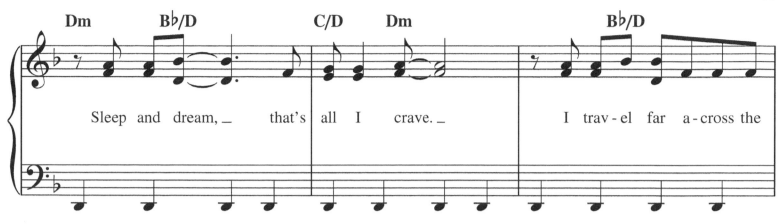

Sleep and dream, _ that's all I crave. _ I trav-el far a-cross the

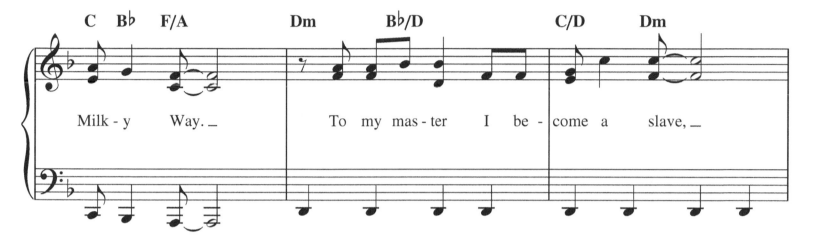

Milk-y Way. _ To my mas-ter I be-come a slave, _

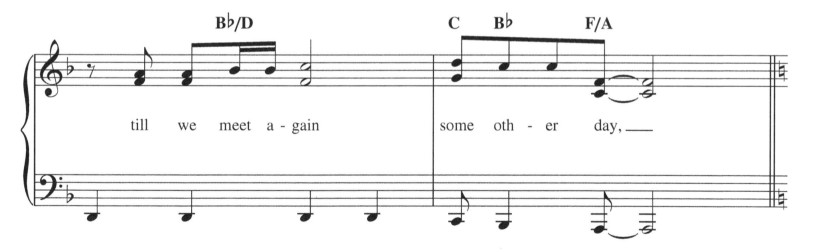

till we meet a-gain some oth-er day, ___

where si-lence speaks _ as loud as war, _ Earth re-turns _ to what it

F   G   C

was be - fore. ____   And then you sense a change, ____

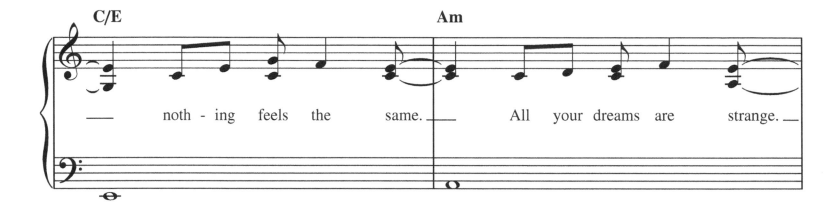

C/E   Am

____ noth - ing feels the same. ____   All your dreams are strange. ____

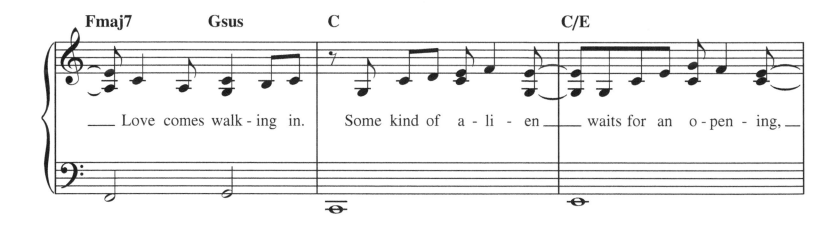

Fmaj7   Gsus   C   C/E

____ Love comes walk - ing in.   Some kind of a - li - en ____ waits for an o - pen - ing, ____

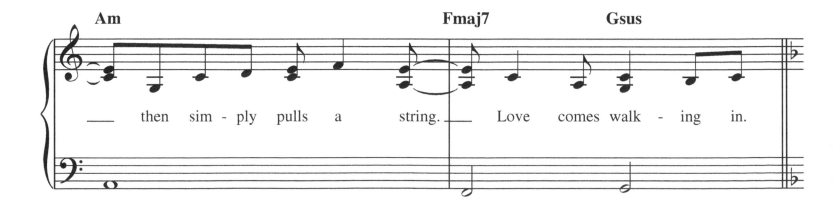

Am   Fmaj7   Gsus

____ then sim - ply pulls a string. ____ Love comes walk - ing in.

Love comes walk - ing in.

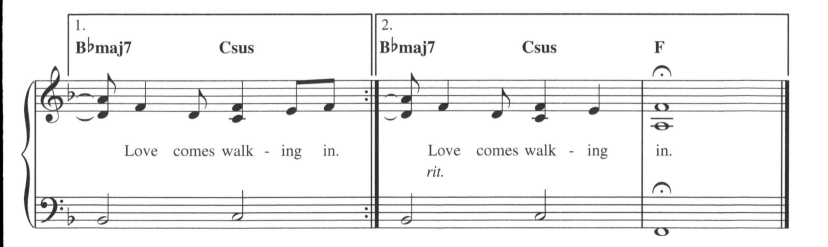

1.

Love comes walk - ing in.

2.

Love comes walk - ing in.

rit.

MOONDANCE

Words and Music by
VAN MORRISON

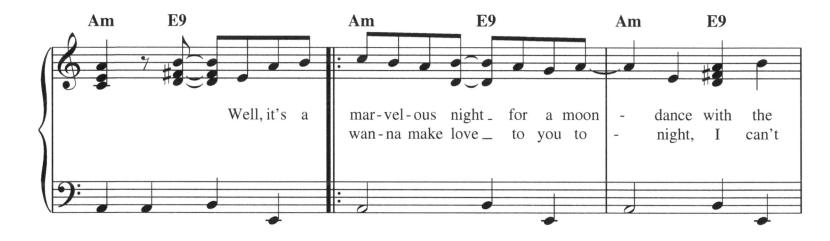

Well, it's a mar-vel-ous night_ for a moon - dance with the
wan-na make love_ to you to - night, I can't

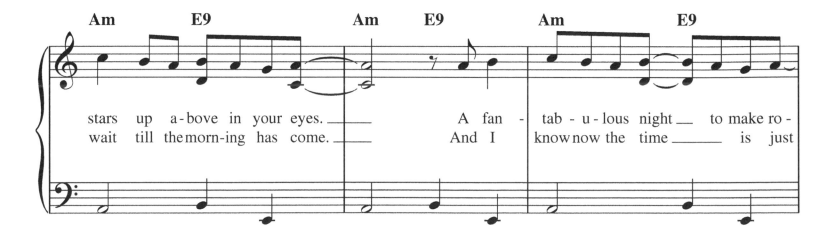

stars up a-bove in your eyes._____
wait till the morn-ing has come._____

A fan - tab-u-lous night_ to make ro -
And I know now the time _____ is just

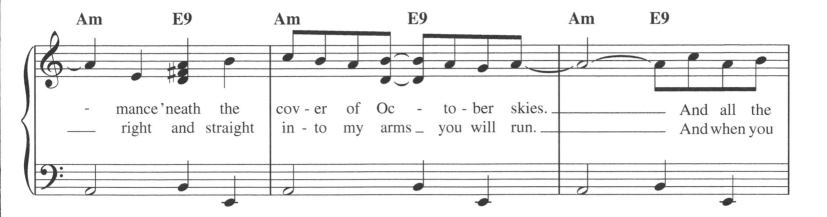

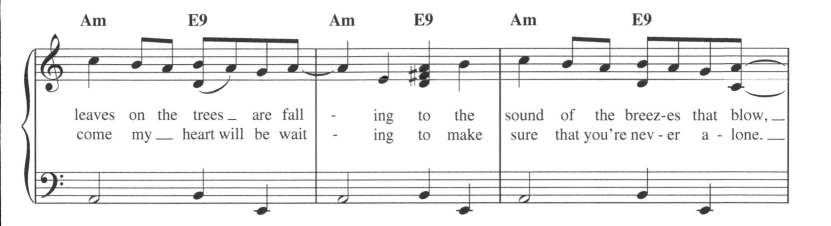

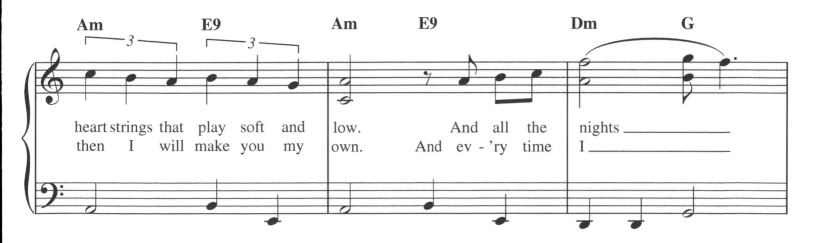

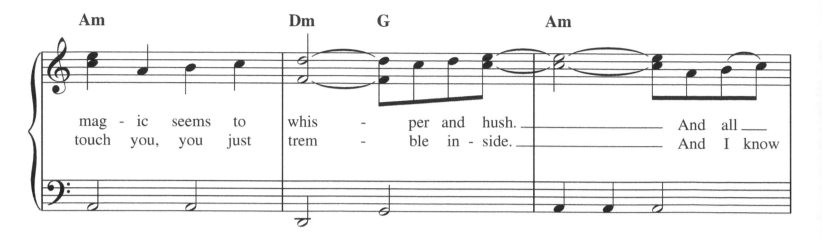

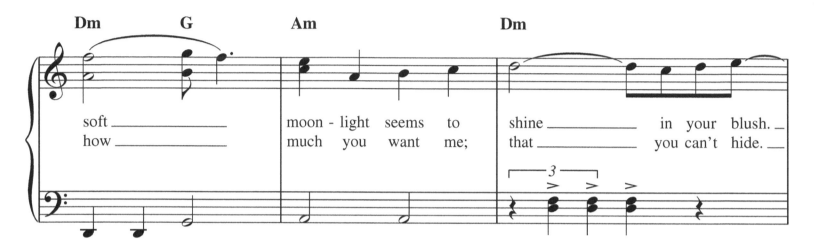

more ro - mance __ with __ you, _____ my love? Well, I

One more moon - dance with you in the

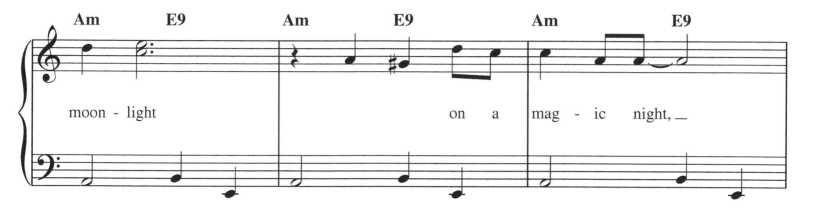

moon - light on a mag - ic night, __

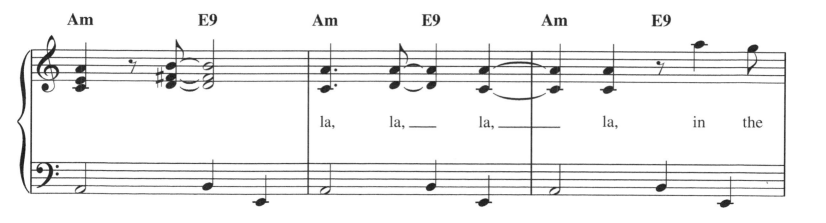

la, la, __ la, ___ la, in the

moon - light　　　　　　　　　on a

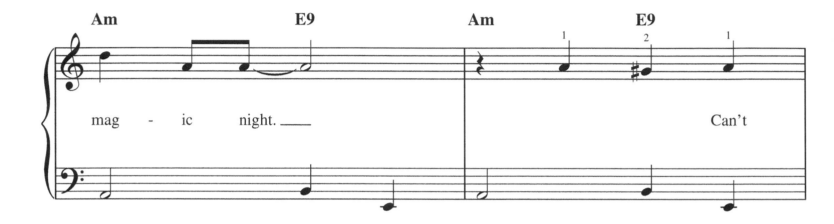

mag - ic night. ____　　　　　Can't

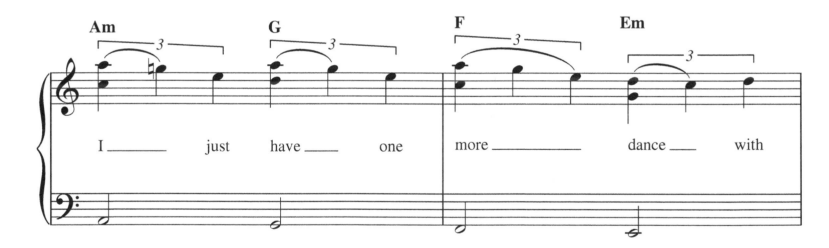

I ____ just have ____ one　　more _____ dance ____ with

you,　　　my ____ love. ____

NOVEMBER RAIN

Words and Music by
W. AXL ROSE

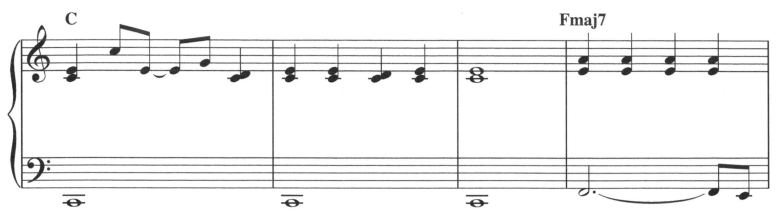

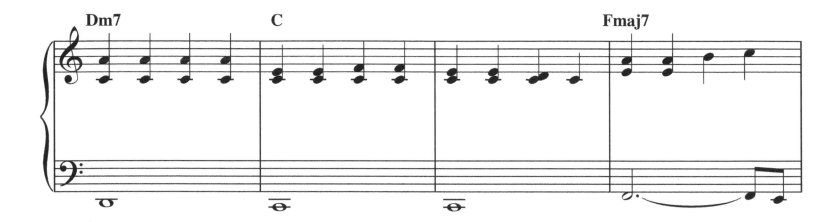

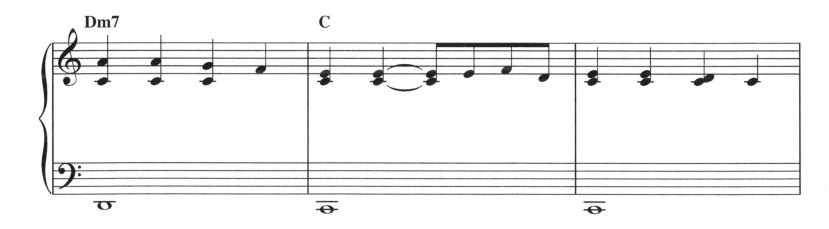

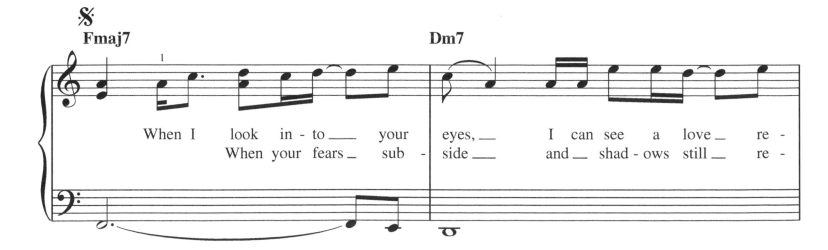

When I look in - to ___ your eyes, ___ I can see a love ___ re -
When your fears ___ sub - side ___ and ___ shad - ows still ___ re -

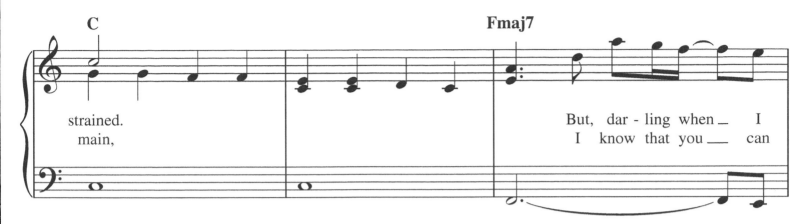

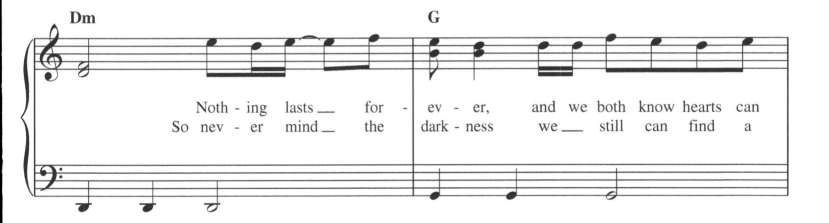

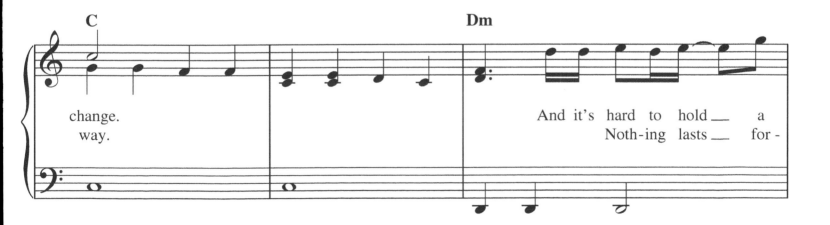

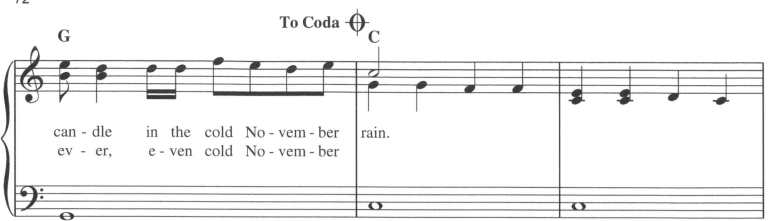

To Coda ⊕

can - dle in the cold No - vem - ber rain.
ev - er, e - ven cold No - vem - ber

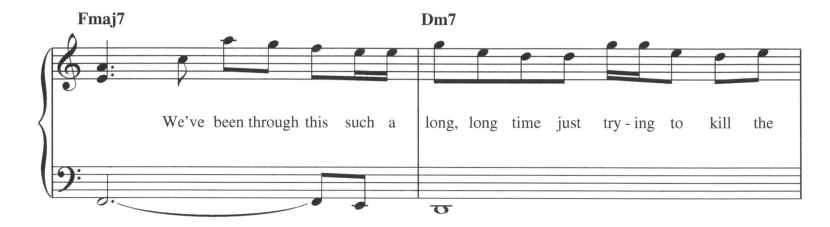

We've been through this such a long, long time just try - ing to kill the

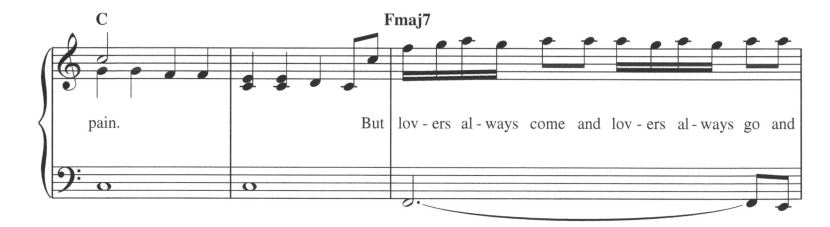

pain. But lov - ers al - ways come and lov - ers al - ways go and

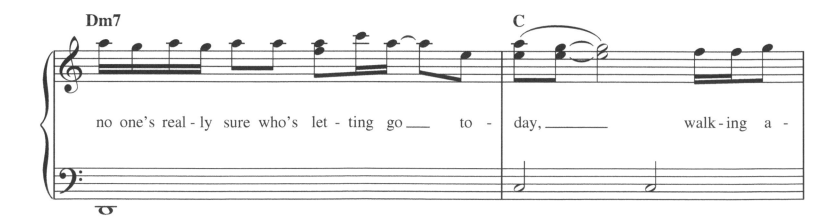

no one's real - ly sure who's let - ting go ___ to - day, _____ walk - ing a -

way. _____ If we could take the time to lay it on the line, I could

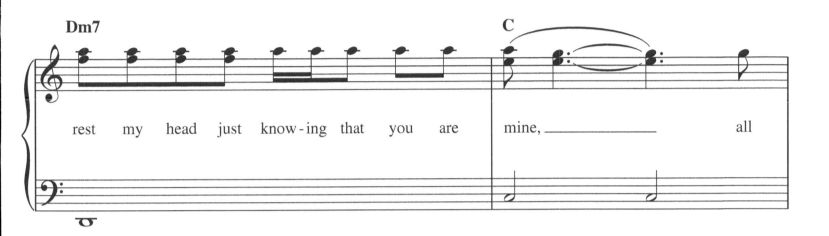

rest my head just know-ing that you are mine, _____ all

mine. ____ So if you wan - na love me, then dar-ling, don't re-

frain, or I'll just end __ up

walk-ing   in the cold No-vem-ber   rain.   Do you

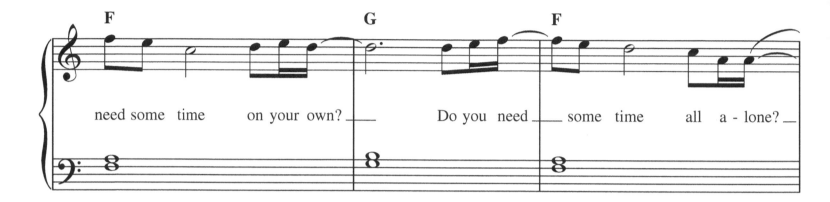

need some time   on your own?____   Do you need____ some time   all a-lone?____

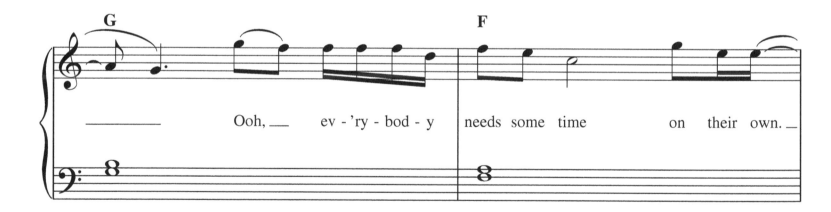

_____   Ooh,___ ev-'ry-bod-y   needs some time   on their own.____

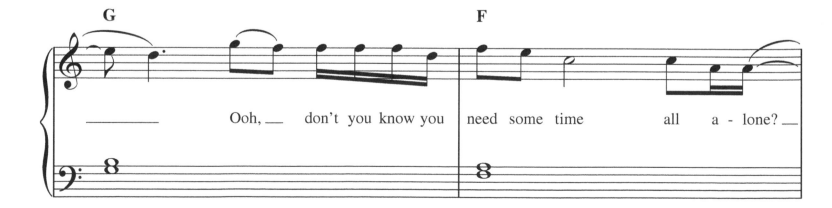

_____   Ooh,___ don't you know you   need some time   all a-lone?____

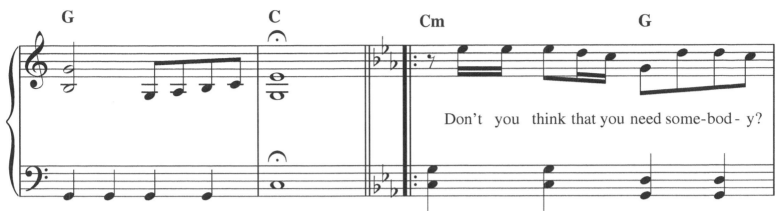

Don't you think that you need some-bod - y?

Don't you think that you need some-one?

Ev-'ry-bod - y needs _ some-bod - y.

You're not the on - ly one. _

You're not the on - ly one. _

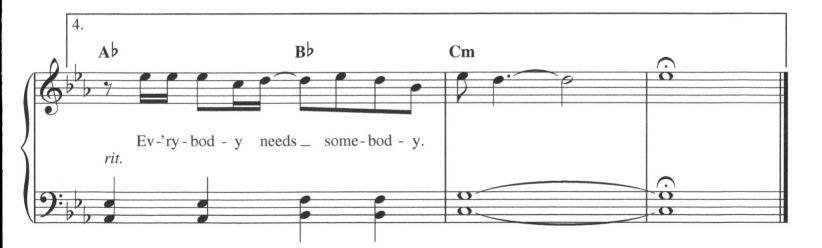

Ev-'ry-bod - y needs _ some-bod - y.

rit.

SHE'S A RAINBOW

Words and Music by MICK JAGGER
and KEITH RICHARDS

Moderately

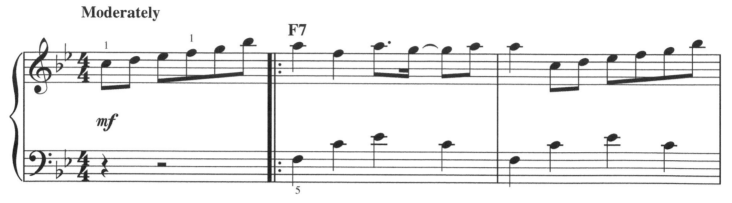

(1., 2.) She comes in col-ors ev-'ry-
(3.) *Instrumental*

where.   She combs her hair.   She's like a rain - bow.

Com-ing, col-ors in the air, oh, ev-'ry - where, she comes in

col - ors.

1., 2.

Instrumental ends

3.

Have you seen her dressed in

blue?
gold,

See the sky in front of you.
like a queen in days of old?

And her face is like a sail, speck of white so fair and
She shoots col - ors all a - round like a sun - set go - ing

pale.
down. Have you seen a la - dy fair - er?

She comes in col - ors ev - 'ry - where. She combs her

hair. She's like a rain - bow. Com - ing, col - ors in the

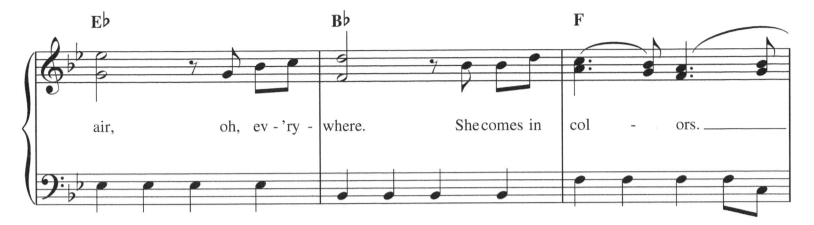

air, oh, ev-'ry-where. She comes in col - ors.___

1.

Have you seen her all in

2.

She's like a rain - bow.

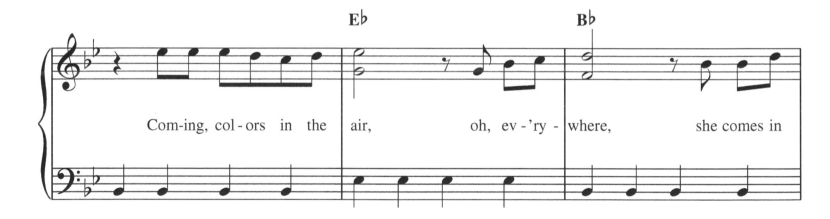

Com-ing, col-ors in the air, oh, ev-'ry - where, she comes in

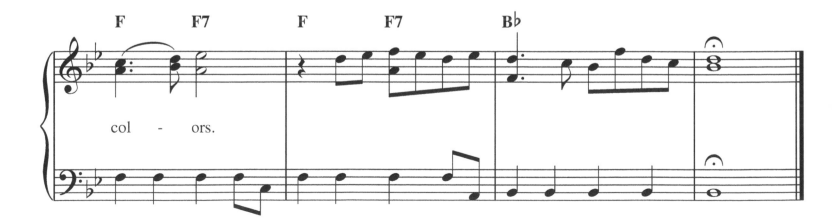

col - ors.

STAIRWAY TO HEAVEN

Words and Music by JIMMY PAGE
and ROBERT PLANT

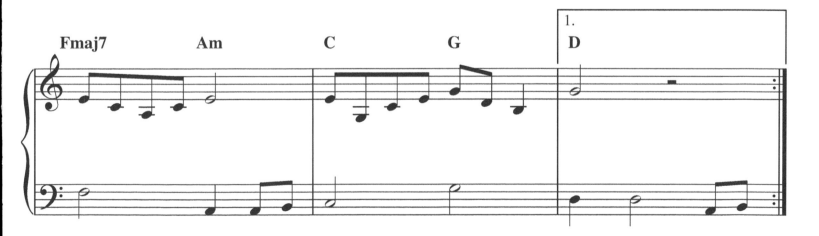

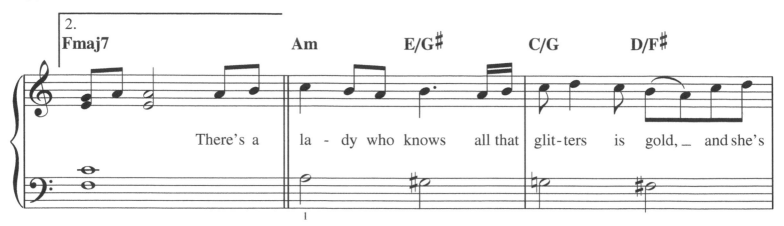

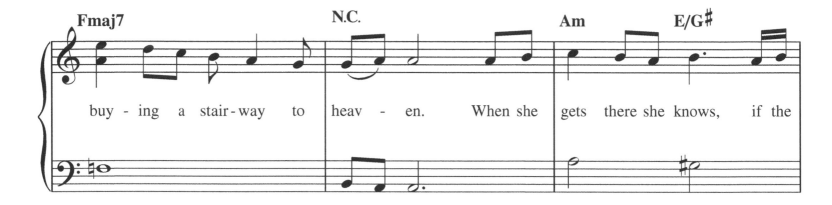

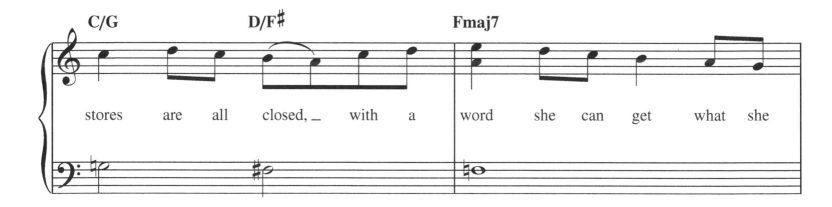

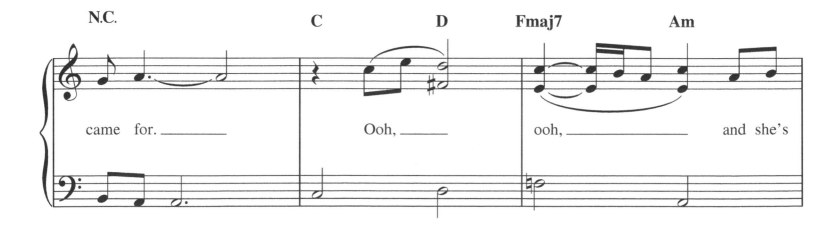

buy - ing a stair - way to heav - en. ____ There's a sign on the wall ____ but she

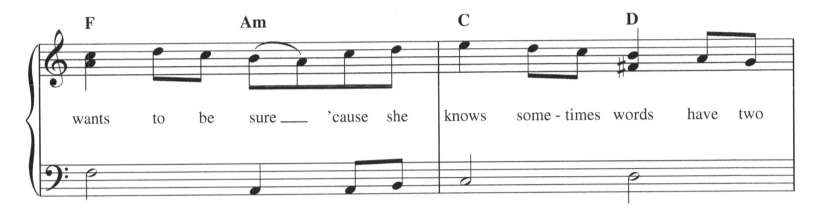

wants to be sure ___ 'cause she knows some - times words have two

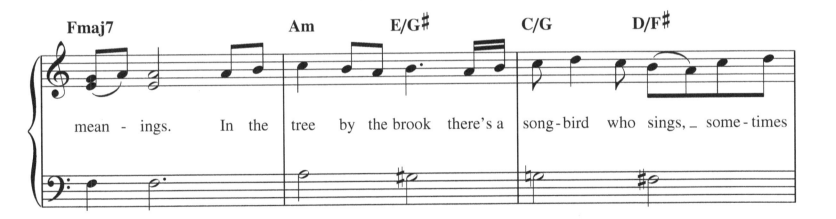

mean - ings. In the tree by the brook there's a song - bird who sings, _ some - times

all of our thoughts are mis - giv - en.

Ooh, it makes me

won - der.

Ooh, _____ it makes me

won - der. __

There's a
And it's

feel - ing I get when I | look to the west, __ and my
whis - pered that soon, if we | all call the tune, __ then the

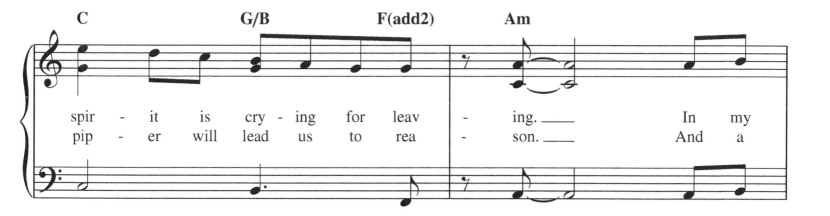

spir - it is cry - ing for leav - ing. __ In my
pip - er will lead us to rea - son. __ And a

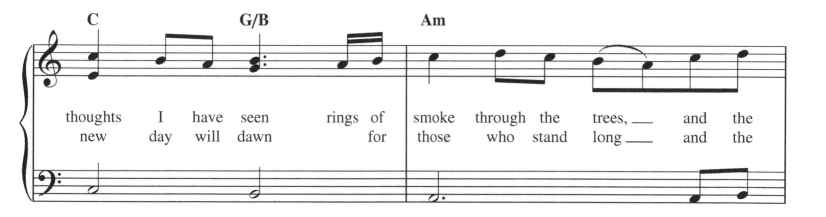

thoughts I have seen rings of | smoke through the trees, __ and the
new day will dawn for | those who stand long __ and the

voic - es of those who stand look - ing. __
for - ests will ech - o with laugh - ter. __

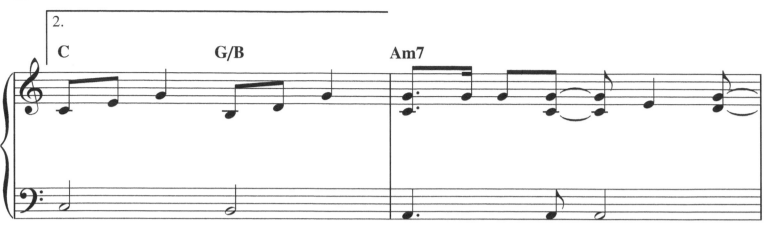

With a strong beat

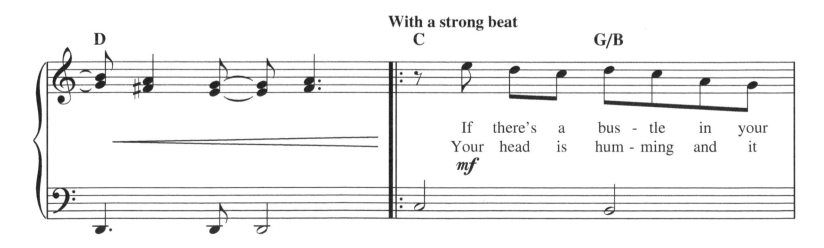

If there's a bus - tle in your
Your head is hum - ming and it

hedge - row ___ don't be a - larmed now,
won't go ___ in case you don't know,

it's just a spring clean for the May
the pip - er's call - ing you to join

Queen. _
him. ___

Yes, there are two paths you can
Dear la - dy, can you hear the

go by, ___ but in the long run,
wind blow, _ and did you know

there's still time to change _ the road
your stair - way lies ___ on ___ the whis -

you're on. ___
p'ring wind? _

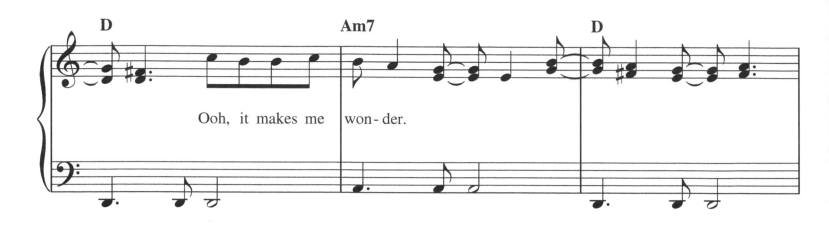

Ooh, it makes me won-der.

Ooh, _____ it makes me won - der. ___

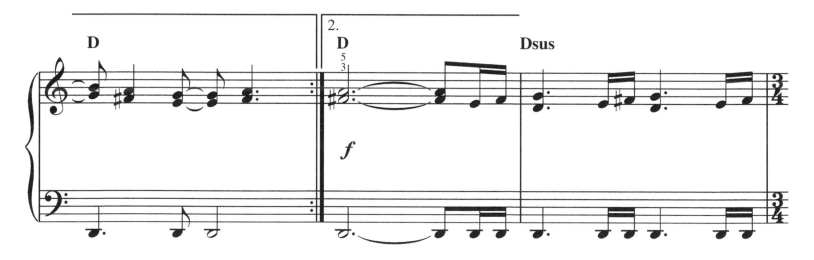

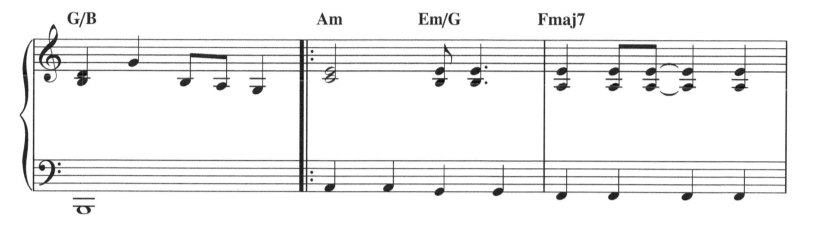

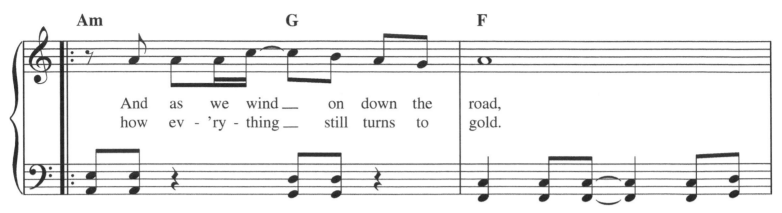

Am   **G**   **F**

And as we wind __ on down the   road,
how ev - 'ry - thing __ still turns to   gold.

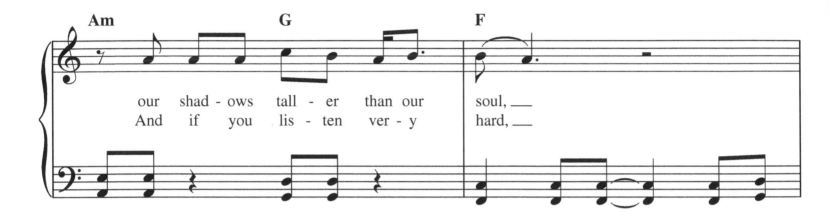

Am   **G**   **F**

our shad - ows tall - er   than our   soul, __
And if you lis - ten ver - y   hard, __

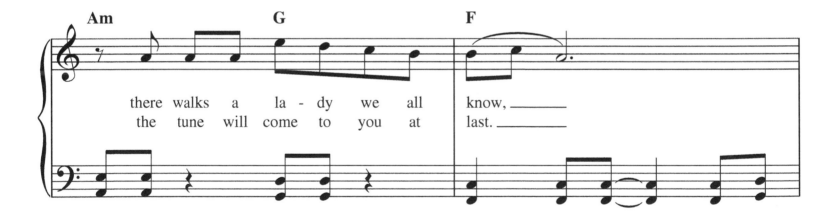

Am   **G**   **F**

there walks a la - dy we all   know, _____
the tune will come to you at   last. _____

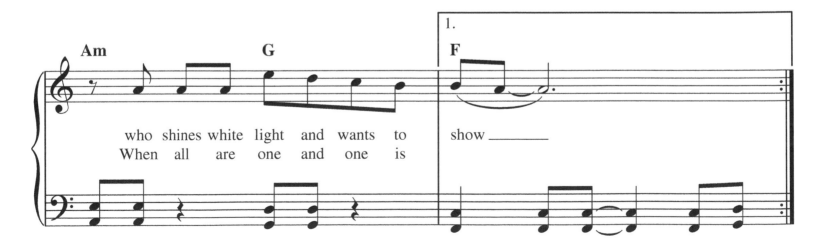

Am   **G**   **1.**
                 F

who shines white light and wants to   show _____
When all are one and one is

SMOKE ON THE WATER

Words and Music by RITCHIE BLACKMORE,
IAN GILLAN, ROGER GLOVER,
JON LORD and IAN PAICE

Heavy Rock beat

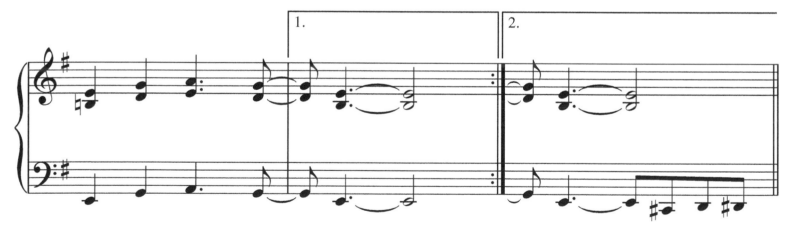

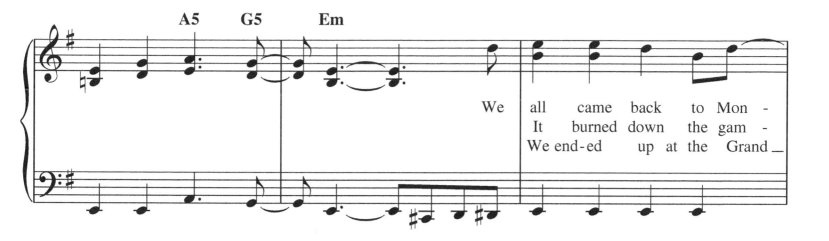

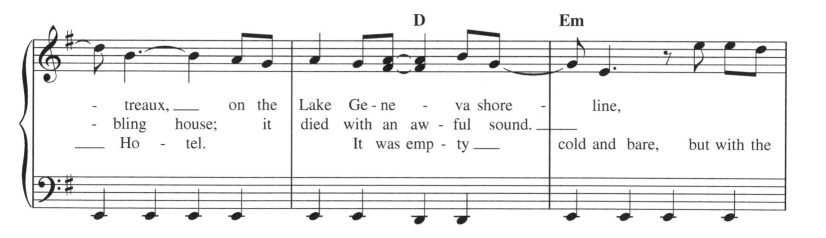

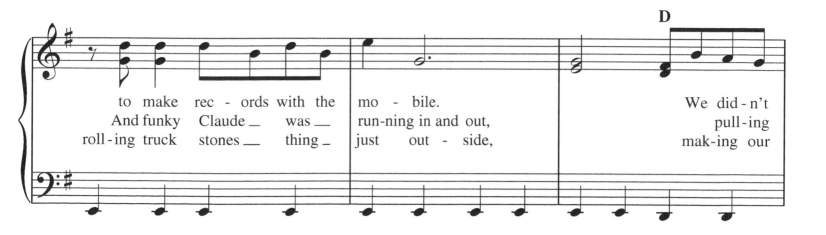

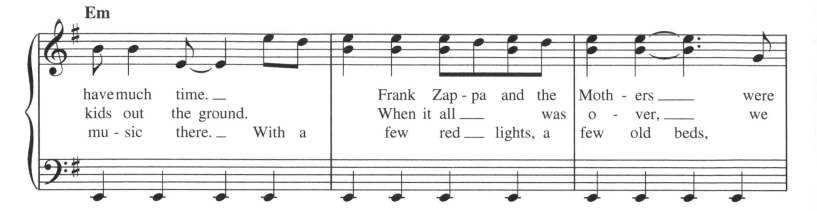

have much time. __
kids out the ground.
mu - sic there. __ With a

Frank Zap - pa and the
When it all __ was
few red __ lights, a

Moth - ers __ were
o - ver, __ we
few old beds,

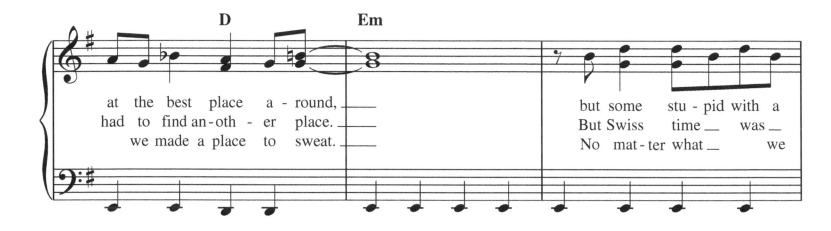

at the best place a - round, __
had to find an-oth - er place. __
we made a place to sweat. __

but some stu - pid with a
But Swiss time __ was __
No mat - ter what __ we

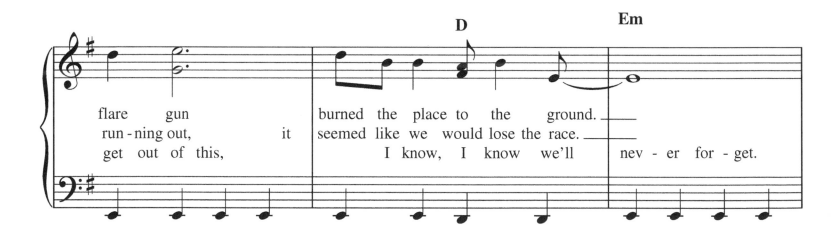

flare gun
run - ning out, it
get out of this,

burned the place to the ground. __
seemed like we would lose the race. __
I know, I know we'll

nev - er for - get.

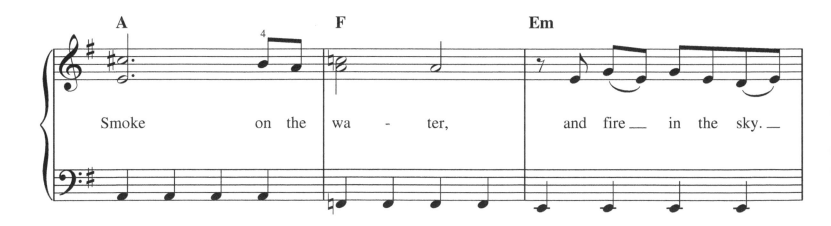

Smoke on the wa - ter,

and fire __ in the sky. __

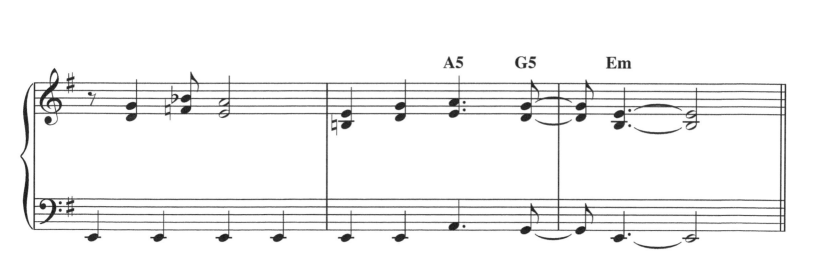

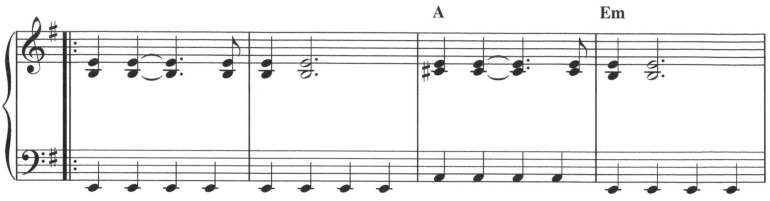

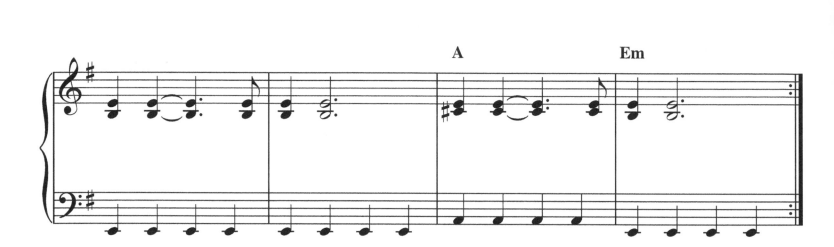

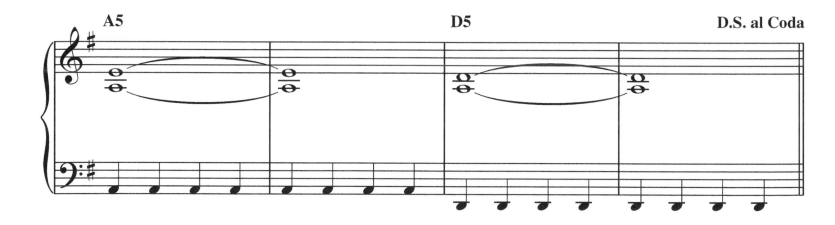

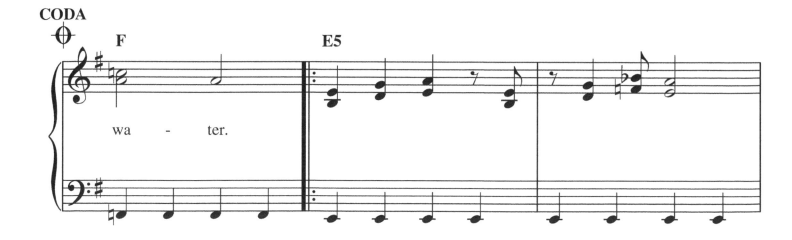

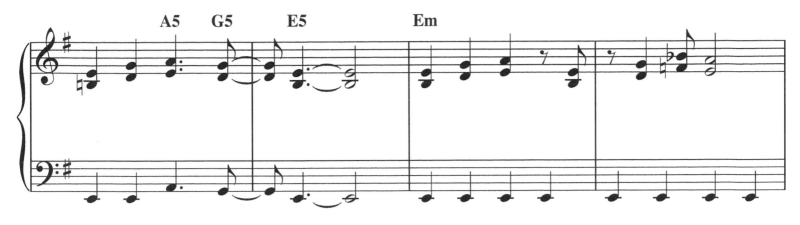

SWEET HOME ALABAMA

Words and Music by RONNIE VAN ZANT,
ED KING and GARY ROSSINGTON

Moderately slow

With pedal

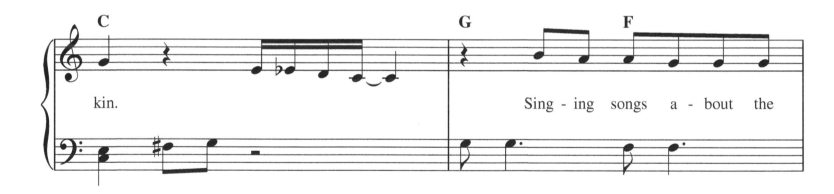

Big wheels keep on turn-ing,   car-ry me home to see my

kin.   Sing - ing songs a - bout the

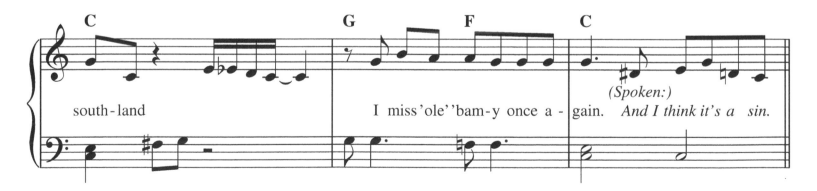

south-land   I miss 'ole' 'bam-y once a - gain. *And I think it's a sin.*

(Spoken:)

Well, I heard Mis-ter Young sing a -

bout her. Well, I heard 'ole Neil put her

down. Well, I hope Neil Young will re -

mem-ber. A south-ern man don't need him a - round an - y-how.

Sweet home Al - a - bam - a,   where the skies   are   so

blue,   sweet home Al - a - bam - a,

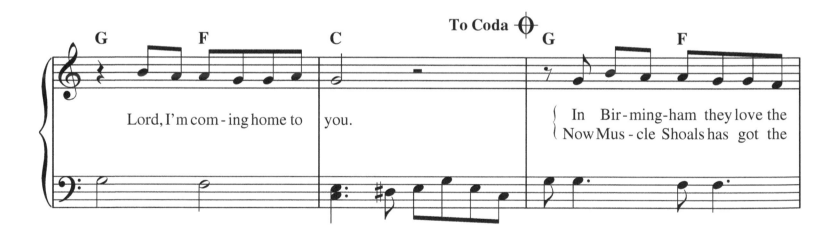

Lord, I'm com - ing home to   you.

In Bir - ming - ham they love the
Now Mus - cle Shoals has got the

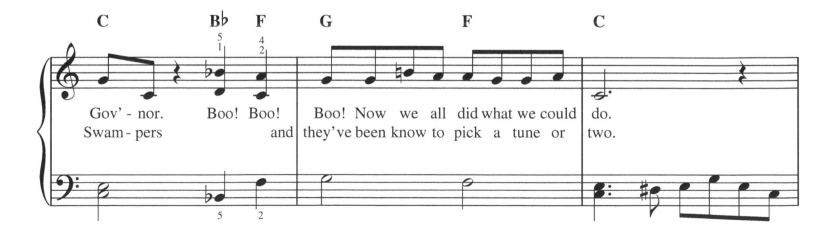

Gov' - nor.   Boo! Boo!   Boo! Now we all did what we could   do.
Swam - pers   and they've been know to pick a tune or   two.

Now Wa - ter - gate does not both - er me.
Lord, _ they get me off so much

Does your con - science both - er
they pick me up when I'm feel - ing

1.

(Spoken:)
you? *Tell the truth.*

2.

D.S. al Coda

(Spoken:)
blue. *Now how about you?*

CODA

Sweet home Al - a -

bam - a,

where the skies are so blue,

sweet home Al - a - bam - a,

Lord, I'm com - ing home to you.

EASY PIANO PLAY-ALONGS
Orchestrated arrangements with you as the soloist!

This series lets you play along with great accompaniments to songs you know and love! Each book comes with recordings of complete professional performances and includes matching custom arrangements in easy piano format. With these books you can: Listen to complete professional performances of each of the songs; Play the easy piano arrangements along with the performances; Sing along with the recordings; Play the easy piano arrangements as solos, without the audio.

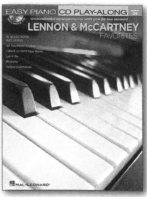

1. GREAT JAZZ STANDARDS
00310916 Book/CD Pack......................................$14.95

2. FAVORITE CLASSICAL THEMES
00310921 Book/CD Pack......................................$14.95

3. BROADWAY FAVORITES
00310915 Book/CD Pack......................................$14.95

4. ADELE
00156223 Book/Online Audio..............................$16.99

5. HIT POP/ROCK BALLADS
00310917 Book/CD Pack......................................$14.95

6. LOVE SONG FAVORITES
00310918 Book/CD Pack......................................$14.95

7. O HOLY NIGHT
00310920 Book/CD Pack......................................$14.95

9. COUNTRY BALLADS
00311105 Book/CD Pack......................................$14.95

11. DISNEY BLOCKBUSTERS
00311107 Book/Online Audio..............................$14.99

12. CHRISTMAS FAVORITES
00311257 Book/CD Pack......................................$14.95

13. CHILDREN'S SONGS
00311258 Book/CD Pack......................................$14.95

15. DISNEY'S BEST
00311260 Book/Online Audio..............................$16.99

16. LENNON & McCARTNEY HITS
00311262 Book/CD Pack......................................$14.95

17. HOLIDAY HITS
00311329 Book/CD Pack......................................$14.95

18. WEST SIDE STORY
00130739 Book/Online Audio $14.99

19. TAYLOR SWIFT
00142735 Book/Online Audio $14.99

20. ANDREW LLOYD WEBBER – FAVORITES
00311775 Book/CD Pack......................................$14.99

21. GREAT CLASSICAL MELODIES
00311776 Book/CD Pack......................................$14.99

22. ANDREW LLOYD WEBBER – HITS
00311785 Book/CD Pack......................................$14.99

23. DISNEY CLASSICS
00311836 Book/CD Pack......................................$14.99

24. LENNON & McCARTNEY FAVORITES
00311837 Book/CD Pack......................................$14.99

26. WICKED
00311882 Book/CD Pack......................................$16.99

27. THE SOUND OF MUSIC
00311897 Book/Online Audio..............................$14.99

28. CHRISTMAS CAROLS
00311912 Book/CD Pack......................................$14.99

29. CHARLIE BROWN CHRISTMAS
00311913 Book/CD Pack......................................$14.99

31. STAR WARS
00110283 Book/Online Audio $16.99

32. SONGS FROM FROZEN, TANGLED AND ENCHANTED
00126896 Book/Online Audio $14.99

Disney characters and artwork © Disney Enterprises, Inc.

Prices, contents and availability subject to change without notice.

FOR MORE INFORMATION, SEE YOUR LOCAL MUSIC DEALER, OR WRITE TO:

HAL•LEONARD®
CORPORATION
7777 W. BLUEMOUND RD. P.O. BOX 13819 MILWAUKEE, WI 53213

www.halleonard.com

0516